Diplomacy Structure
and
Action

Rules of Preparing Diplomatic Calibers

Era of Modern Management
HR. Sustainable Development

Ibrahim H. Hussney

Accredited Lecturer and Instructor

"Investing in building human beings is now at the top of the pyramid of states' concerns as the most important industry in this information age, as a result of nations realizing that their fate and future will always depend on the creativity of their citizens, and the extent of their challenge and response towards change always for the better....!!!!"

CONTENTS

Diplomacy is structure and action

The fact indicates that diplomacy as a human practice is deeply rooted in history, as its emergence coincided with the birth of man and the formation of groups on this earth, and over time its concepts evolved. Diplomacy is characterized by interaction and movement and it is a natural reflection of the movement of human groups in their dealings with each other to regulate and control the relationships between themselves.

Diplomacy has gone in the history through many developments in terms of concepts and nature, the nature of diplomacy has moved from temporary and unstable cases to permanent cases, from individual (personal) diplomacy to parliamentary diplomacy, and from the nature that is characterized by secret to the public nature, from bilateral diplomacy to multilateral diplomacy, and from diplomacy with one dimension to diplomacy with multiple dimensions, and finally from diplomacy that is not codified to diplomacy that is regulated by treaties and international agreements.

Speaking about contemporary diplomacy approaches, we will find that they are of great importance, as they play a prominent role in the field of international relations and foreign affairs of states in their political, economic, social, cultural, and other newly developed fields, and the pursuit of adopting the diplomacy approach is reflected through the desire of the member states of society, the international establishment of diplomatic relations and the exchange of representatives of diplomatic and consular missions with each other, and this matter also applies to representatives of international and regional organizations and all members of international law.

From the foregoing, we will find that diplomatic approaches have become today the main tool for implementing and following up the foreign policies of countries that have been applied by modern tools and systems of governance that are based on democracy, pluralism, parliamentary life, and political participation.

Thus, diplomacy is generally considered the art of managing and directing international relations through dialogue and negotiation, which is carried out by staff in the diplomatic corps to manage crises and settle disputes by peaceful means.

Also, modern diplomacy is playing a major and effective role in the economic development, the protection of human rights, the preservation of environmental protection, the dialogue of religions and civilizations, and others, to serve the interests of states, achieving their goals, and bringing them closer together.

In the end, it must be noted the growing role played by contemporary diplomacy in the field of strengthening friendly relations between countries, encouraging cooperation among them, and contributing to resolving and settling disputes, as we mentioned previously, which reflects positively on international peace and security.

In addition to the important functions that diplomatic and consular missions perform in the field of protecting and caring for the interests of states and their nationals, and mainly participating in preparing the directions and paths of foreign policies for these countries through the information they provide to decision-makers and presidents, kings, and princes of states, diplomacy is structure and action.

The beginnings of diplomacy

The origin of the word diplomacy and its phased development

Diplomacy is a word of Greek origin, and it refers to the document issued by officials or leaders and heads of cities that grant its bearer certain privileges, and in the era of Roman civilization, it was the word that referred to the folded document that could be folded and carried from one place to another.

The meaning of diplomacy in the era of the Roman Empire

Diplomacy in this era was a reference to express the natures of ambassadors or envoys, as it referred to all the instructions that the diplomatic mission had to follow and abide by about the ethics of the profession and the development of ways of friendship with other countries and distance from motives of criticism, as indicated by diplomacy in this era as well to the content of the official certificate or document that includes the rights of the envoy, the mission he is coming to, and the recommendations issued in this regard by the governor of a town or his region to present him, welcoming him well, and facilitate his movements between the different regions of the host country.

The date and place of birth of the word diplomacy

Diplomacy is the word that has been circulated in the United Kingdom since the date of 1796 AD, until today, to denote the management of international relations, which was also applied to the representatives of foreign countries accredited to it.

Modern meanings and concepts of the diplomatic profession

According to modern concepts, the profession of diplomacy has acquired many meanings and similes that have been given to it, such as resourcefulness and intelligence, the science of relations, a means of negotiation, a profession of a special nature, a human style, a means of primary defense, a synonym for politics, a ballad, work management, art and interests, science and action, a title for organizations, cunning, monitoring, and protection, is synonymous with politics.

Concept and definition of contemporary diplomacy

It is a continuous political process that countries formally employ towards implementing their foreign policy and managing their relations with other countries and international bodies.

Areas of diplomatic action

The fields of diplomatic work are diverse and complementary between being a mechanism for representation to others, a mechanism for negotiation on behalf of the state, a mechanism for strengthening all kinds of relations between countries, a means for gathering information about the host country, and a means for protecting the interests of the country and its citizens.

Mechanism of representation to others

Diplomacy is the mechanism that refers to the permanent or temporary actual presence of a country (resident or non-resident mission) in another country by participating in the activities and affairs of the protocol, ceremonies, and events of the host country, and such a presence takes upon itself the means of presenting the policies of the country it represents and clarifying its elements and directions and defense about her.

The negotiation mechanism on behalf of the state

The diplomatic mission follows the mechanism of negotiation with the host country on behalf of the government of its country, with the aim of reaching a settlement, reconciliation, agreement or concluding a treaty within the framework that achieves the interest of the two parties and maintains the permanent good relations between them.

Mechanism for strengthening relations between countries

Among the basic tasks of diplomatic missions is to strengthen existing relations with host and accredited countries, by opening horizons for new areas of coordination and cooperation by maximizing positive elements of common interest between the two countries.

A means of collecting information about the host countries

For the country's government to make its decisions regarding the host country for its accredited mission, this mission must provide its government with all information about the host country's conditions politically, economically, socially, etc., and prepare reports on these matters in the presence of the necessary assessment and analysis.

A means to protect the interests of the country and the citizens of its subjects

Diplomacy is a means to protect the interests of the country and its nationals in the countries accredited to it, to work to develop those interests by all legitimate means, and to defend the security of the country represented by the mission and protect it from external threats and monitor all treaties concluded with the host countries.

The concept of
traditional diplomacy

Evolving of diplomacy concept through the ages

The starting point for the development of the primitive diplomatic concept was its origin in ancient times, then this path took a way between ancient civilizations, such as the Indian civilization, the Chinese civilization, and the Pharaonic civilization. Then the era of the Messenger (PBUH) and the Rightly Guided Caliphate, then the era of the Umayyad state, the era of the Abbasid state, the era of kingdoms and emirates, the era of the Islamic state, and finally the modern era.

The concept of traditional diplomacy, its origin, and development

It is a kind of diplomacy that was characterized by secrecy, as it continued to be practiced from the fifteenth century AD until the outbreak of the First World War, and it relied on the principle of permanent diplomatic representation, and the Papal Chair was the first to initiate the establishment of the permanent mission's system.

Then came the Treaty of Westphalia of 1648, which approved the principle of the balance of power for the first time in the world, which prompted countries to establish permanent diplomatic missions to monitor each other, and permanent diplomatic exchange after the French Revolution became one of the rights established for every sovereign state.

This was followed by the Vienna Conference of 1815, which approved the established rules for building modern diplomacy as a profession in which the envoy represents his country and not the ruler. This refers to the independence of the ambassador who enjoys competence, which makes him a contributor to the preparation and implementation of the foreign policy of his country.

The best models of traditional diplomacy

Features of traditional Italian diplomacy

Venice's diplomacy flourished until the middle of the eighteenth century when it was the most famous Italian state in this field as a result of the wisdom and sophistication of its ambassadors, and it established missions for it in France, Spain, England, and some European countries, and other states headed the same path as Milan sent a permanent mission to Genoa in 1455, then a mission Permanent to Rome in 1460.

The instructions issued to the ambassadors were in two bodies, either public about documenting political and commercial relations, or secret about sources of information gathering, making deals, and caring for the interests of the state.

Machiavellianism settled in the conscience of political thought as an expression of "the end justifies the means", and as Machiavelli mentioned in his book "The Prince" lived through this era, where he called for the right of the absolute ruler to take the necessary steps to maintain his rule and impose his control away from a commitment to any kind of morality, as if he resorts to lies, cunning and deceit.

Features of traditional French diplomacy

In the seventeenth century AD, Cardinal Richelieu, through his distinguished course towards the development of diplomacy, established the first permanent central body for drawing up a foreign policy to track negotiations and supervise the establishment of permanent and stable relations, and as a result, permanent embassies of France spread in the most important European countries, and the French language emerged as a language of communication since the eighteenth-century AD.

Among the most important diplomatic principles established by Cardinal Richelieu is considering that negotiations as a permanent profession entrusted to one minister to increase efficiency, work to educate public opinion about the state's foreign policy and its goals, work to study the terms of treaties carefully during negotiation, and adhere to and respect what is agreed upon.

Also, he calls to put the interest of the state before any consideration and permits the state to enter into alliances with other countries to serve this interest, and the consideration of diplomacy has become a continuous approach that aims to reach permanent agreements that lead to the establishment of strong relations with others.

Indeed, in this era, all specializations related to foreign relations became part of the work of the Ministry of Foreign Affairs, which was established in 1626 AD.

The most important changes that occurred in the traditional diplomacy

By the end of the nineteenth century and the beginning of the twentieth century AD, the public opinion of the peoples of most European countries played an important role in shaping the internal and foreign policy that turned into a democratic system, which helped push diplomacy toward more publicity and gaining popularity.

With time, diplomacy has become an important factor in curbing the increasing influence of European countries with their many and huge capabilities, which facilitated their control over the capabilities of small countries under the banner of balancing international powers and their responsibility towards maintaining world peace.

And let's not forget the scientific and technical progress, especially in the fields of communication and transportation, which led to an increase and ease of communication between European countries and the growth and prosperity of common interests between them, which increased the importance of seeking to modernize and develop the rules of inter-diplomatic relations.

The most important characteristics of traditional diplomacy

*- The spread of what is called summit diplomacy among the leaders of states.

*- Increasing the importance of granting diplomatic immunities and privileges to workers in this field.

*- The continued use of the secret diplomacy approach in negotiating and concluding treaties and agreements.

*- Increasing interest in protocol aspects, ceremonies, and the precedence of arrangements in meetings and celebrations.

*- Limiting diplomatic representation to countries only, or bilateral representation due to the absence of international organizations.

*- The adoption of the system of permanent missions by European countries on their lands in the presence of the development of some rules of representation.

The main disadvantages of traditional diplomacy

One of the most important factors that point to the shortcomings of traditional diplomacy is what Dr. Hans Morgenthau said in the twentieth century AD:

*- Traditional diplomacy contradicts the principles of democracy, so diplomacy must be unveiled and all its details are known.

*- Traditional diplomacy with its bodies is considered useless and is a waste of time and inconsistent due to its compromise of ethical principles.

*- Traditional diplomacy is responsible for the political disasters that befell humanity during the stages in which it was prevalent, and it is logical that methods that prove to be incorrect should be replaced.

Stages of development of the diplomatic industry

What we can express with regard to the old image of diplomacy revolves around messages exchanged between the rulers of kingdoms, regions, and tribes, with regard to good neighborliness, spreading peace, preparing for war, or settling problems and disputes, which used to come in the form of what was copied and written on a piece of paper, leather, or on a wooden board, or on tree leaves, or papyrus paper...etc.

The modern shape of diplomacy

One of the most prominent features of the modern shape of diplomacy is its great interest in both jobs and interests, and this was evident in the discussions of the attendees at the Vienna Conference held in 1815, in order to settle issues arising from the French Revolutionary, the Napoleonic Wars, the disintegration of the Roman Empire, and redrawing the political map of the continent European.

Contemporary shape of diplomacy

One of the most prominent features of the contemporary shape of diplomacy is its great interest in each of the methods and ceremonies (protocol), and this was evident in the discussions of the attendees at the Paris Conference in 1919, which was held for reconciliation between the victorious parties in the First World War and the defeated parties, as it resulted in this conference, The Treaty of Versailles with its severe penalties for the defeated countries.

Attributes of modern diplomacy according to its rules

The two most important rules that distinguish the features of modern diplomacy are **method and practice**. Modern methods have led to providing the required ease for the work of a diplomat and shortening the time for decision-making as a result of shrinking time distances and borders between countries, and tremendous progress in the fields of communication technology, transportation, information circulation, and news.

As for practice, this led to the birth of the method of overt diplomacy and the reduction of the role of secret diplomacy due to the expansion of democratic regimes, the supremacy of liberal regimes, the promotion of popular participation, and the consideration of public opinion when drawing up state policies.

Secret style in diplomatic work

We can say that diplomacy is not an open book that can be viewed by everyone, at any time, as diplomacy is governed by some controls regarding the principle of secrecy, and here we have to differentiate between the concept of secret diplomacy and the concept of secret negotiations.

Secret diplomacy

It is the type that sponsors secret negotiations between two states or a group of states, in order to finally reach the conclusion of treaties and agreements that are secret, which are often related to the distribution of spheres of influence and control during the era of conquests, expansion, occupation, and colonies.

Secret negotiations

The confidential nature of the negotiations may be required during the stages preceding reaching the final results that will be signed. It is unreasonable for public opinion to become aware of all stages of the negotiations, which could prevent a convergence of views between countries on many issues of international relations.

Features of contemporary diplomacy
(advanced diplomacy)

*- Adoption of the principle of equality in sovereignty between states from a legal point of view.

*- Follow the method of public diplomacy, and seek to eliminate the confidentiality of treaties and the right of peoples to self-determination.

*- Relentlessly striving towards improving relations between countries by encouraging the spirit of tolerance and promoting the idea of understanding and friendly cooperation between countries.

"This is what is emphasized by the Charter of the United Nations"

Factors shaping the structure of modern international relations

In order to reach a better understanding of the factors shaping the structure of international relations, it is necessary to resort to the differentiation between the contradictions. We see that there is what is called the diplomacy of the East, which is faced on the other side by the diplomacy of the West, and there is the capitalist system, which is faced by the communist regime, and dictatorial regimes, which are faced by democratic regimes, and there is the diplomacy of axes and alliances, which is faced by the diplomacy of neutrality and non-alignment.

This diversity and differentiation, in addition to the increase in the international representation of different civilizations, cultures, values, and political beliefs, all of this led to the complexity and intertwining of international dealings as a result of the existence of different interests, goals, and ideologies within the international community.

Diplomacy and its connection to international concepts

The relationship between diplomacy and foreign policy

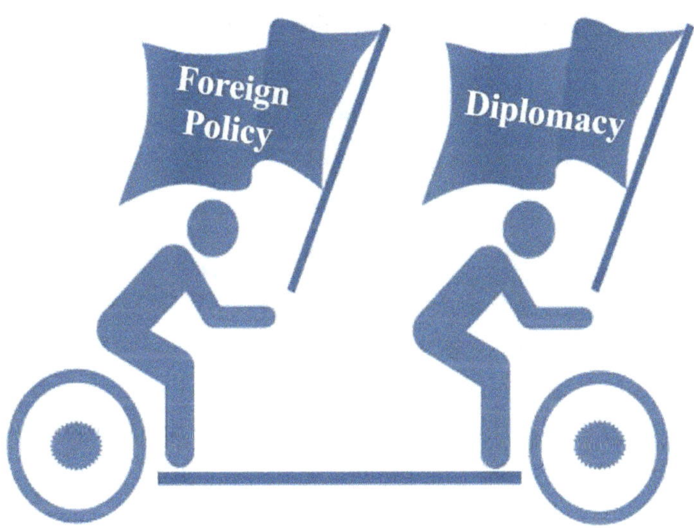

Diplomacy plays a leading, important, and pivotal role in helping to draw up the foreign policy of the state, as it is considered a mechanism for preparing foreign policy and a tool for its implementation. It is also a tool for presenting the state's policies, clarifying its elements and directions, and defending them.

The relationship between diplomacy and public policy of the state

The foreign policy represents plans, actions, and the approach that the state follows in its political, economic, and strategic relations with other countries. It is an essential part of the state's general policy and expresses the will of the people. Diplomacy is the main means of implementing the state's foreign policy and achieving its goals in times of peace and war.

Overlap between diplomacy and foreign policy

The foreign policy of the state cannot become successful without a deep understanding of the objectives of this policy and its elaborate implementation from the most prominent members of the diplomatic bodies of the state.

Ministry of Foreign Affairs is considered an essential element in collecting and evaluating information and status and conditions of other countries and preparing reports for the decision-maker that reflects the general political frameworks of the state, and by virtue of this nature, the Ministry of Foreign Affairs is considered a decisive factor towards drawing up the foreign policy of the state.

Titles of the goals of international relations between states

The titles of goals to be reached through the existing relations between states vary between achieving certain objectives, preserving interests, facing challenges, protecting against threats, or achieving targets at the political, economic, commercial, cultural, or environmental, or military, so international relations is a multi-faceted process of interaction between two or more countries, to varying degrees.

Diplomacy in its professional sense is a specialized body that represents the state to manage its foreign relations with other countries in the light of different interests or their similarity, as the goal of this is to serve and succeed the state's foreign policy and achieve its goals and interests within the limits of available resources and capabilities, and therefore diplomacy and international relations meet to achieve the interests of states and preserve their national security.

Modern trucks of international relations

In addition to the traditional form of diplomacy that we have been accustomed to for many years, a number of modern tracks affecting international relations have been added to this form in which diplomatic action has been involved, such as national liberation movements, non-governmental organizations, giant international companies, regional and international organizations, and the investments in different fields.

Diplomacy and its relation to international law

In general, international law is divided into two parts, customary international law, and international convention law, and in connection with that, we will find that diplomatic relations and customs played a major role in shaping international law with the source of customary and conventions, and the legal rules that relate to diplomacy and the organization of its work have become part of international law that It is called diplomatic law.

Diplomatic law is a branch of international law that is concerned with regulating external communication between states and the means of representing them to others. It is also concerned with how to manage international affairs, consultation, and negotiation.

Factors for developing contemporary diplomacy methods

*- The emergence of new tasks in addition to diplomatic work.

*- Increasing and multiplying the components of the international community.

*- Breadth of interdependence and concern for common interests between countries.

*- The modern industrial revolution and its impact on the means of communication and transportation.

*- Increasing the influence of local and international public opinion on the decision-maker and diplomatic action.

*- The unprecedented and rapid progress in the technical field, and the birth of multiple modern technologies.

* The growing number of international organizations and agencies and the widening and diversification of their work and activities.

Increasing and multiplying the components of the international community

The steady increase in the number of countries that gained their independence and joined the international community through their membership in international organizations, especially the United Nations, led to the identification of different civilizations, religions, races, beliefs, and political ideologies, which led to the expansion of the scope of diplomatic communication and the growth of the negotiation mechanism, which is the matter added qualitative dimensions to the concept of diplomacy in its broadest sense.

The pillar of interdependence and the importance of common interests

The nature of the current era has imposed a growing sense among different countries of common destiny and has produced what we can call the intertwining of interests among the peoples of those countries, which confirms the inability of any single country to become self-sufficient in facing the challenges from its position in the international environment.

The transition of the usual method of diplomacy from a one-sided diplomacy mechanism that focuses on achieving the foreign policy goals of states in a way that achieves their interests and only, to a multi-faceted diplomacy mechanism that is concerned with managing international relations and achieving common goals of global concern, such as combating environmental pollution and fighting organized crime, and forms of violence, extremism, and terrorism in all their forms, dealing with the effects of the population explosion, treating the effects of poverty, hunger, and disease, providing food, and limiting the spread of weapons of mass destruction...etc.

The impact of the modern industrial revolution and technological advances

The modern industrial revolution, with all its components, innovative manufacturing methods, and modern technologies, especially in the fields of transportation and communications, allowed broader fields and dimensions, and added speed and flexibility to the mechanisms of negotiation and decision-making, as a result of freedom and ease of movement, the emergence of the mobile diplomatic envoy, and the speed of settling matters from the decision-maker, and the shift from the mechanism of indirect diplomacy to the mechanism of direct diplomacy.

The emergence of new tasks and the decline of old ones

If we look closely at the history of diplomatic missions, we will be able to identify two types of diplomacy, the first type refers to what is called clean diplomacy, and the second type is called dirty diplomacy.

The first type is concerned with and is involved in international trade agreements, organizing international navigation, offering initiatives to establish peace and resolve disputes, and concluding treaties and agreements to preserve the environment, we can see that this type of diplomacy in today's world growing and expanding.

While dirty diplomacy is that diplomacy that reflected the Cold War, works to stir up unrest, spread rumors, and espionage, and perhaps also pave the way for military intervention, today this type of diplomacy is in decline.

The growing number of international organizations and its impact on countries

International organizations are considered an incubator for small countries, in order to increase the scope of their diplomatic representation.

Through these organizations, the so-called bilateral diplomacy has grown between countries, and the presence of these organizations has worked to add various international activities, such as human rights, crime control, protection of the environment and population, the comprehensive development of societies, international intervention for humanitarian purposes, and the impact of the presence of these organizations did not stop at this point, but also helped in the growth of what is called multilateral diplomacy.

Diplomatic features within international organizations

Bilateral diplomacy

Knowledge and familiarity with the rules and procedures and the ability to defend, initiate and plead, and it is a work that requires personal skills characterized by maneuvering and seizing opportunities to achieve interests or minimize damages.

Multilateral diplomacy

This type of diplomacy includes fact-finding missions, provision of services and expertise, provision of aid to reach solutions, resorting to mediation, arbitration, investigation and conciliation, and collective pressure required on a country, which are actions that are carried out through multiple and disparate frameworks and require different skills and specializations.

The effects of domestic and international public opinion

*- Local public opinion's interest in political decisions and government actions and policies.

*- The governments of countries realize the importance of sympathy, which may amount to support for their policies towards managing crises and facing the challenges and risks facing the country.

*- Increasing popular control over the state's foreign policy, stemming from the people's conviction that the outputs of this policy are reflected negatively or positively on their destinies, their livelihood, and the level of well-being they aspire to.

*- The pressure of international public opinion also constitutes an important tributary towards correcting the policies of some countries' governments when local public opinion fails to do so, as it is weak in the face of the domination and intransigence of these governments.

International changes and the new world order

A number of global events during the past century had a great impact on the birth of the variables that led to the formation of the new world order that we see today.

These variables began to appear after the end of the Cold War, the collapse of the Berlin Wall, the Gulf War 90/91, and the dissolution of the Soviet Union, this was followed by the emergence of giant economic blocs, which eventually led to the birth of economic unilateralism, based on the free capitalist system identified with market mechanisms.

From here, we can identify the titles of the essential changes in international relations, which included, the decline in the scope of state power in exchange for globalization, the different direction of the compass of priorities in the countries of the world, the emergence of the effects of scientific development and contemporary technological progress, the obscurity of the issue of control and hegemony, and the growing issue of economic and technological capabilities.

The decline of the scope of state power in exchange for globalization

In light of the phenomenon of globalization, the absolute authority of the state has become restricted due to its close connection with global and regional institutions, their principles, and the foundations according to which they operate, foremost of that is the penetration of economic networks the border of countries and establishing their markets with different ideas, principles, and interests that may conflict with what the relevant state authority desires.

Directions of the countries' compasses priorities became different

The emergence of a clear difference in the direction of the compass of countries' priorities from the previous direction, as the old-world order was suffering under the weight of the effects of the Cold War, the arms race, and ideological and regional conflicts.

While the features of the priorities of the new world order direct their compass towards treating the problem of unemployment in all countries at the world level, following up on currency rates, solving environmental and pollution problems, and developing ways of communication and contacts.

The results of the intensification of the conflict of priorities in the countries

With the transformation of states from the old (totalitarian) world order to the new (democratic) world order, and with the development of means of communication and contacts, there are not many authoritarian governments left with many means to hide facts or shortcomings from local and international public opinion, just as the values of democracy and human rights have become it finds remarkable popularity in the newly transformed countries.

The effects of scientific development and contemporary technological progress

The effects of scientific development and contemporary technological progress stem from each of the contemporary third industrial revolutions, and the endless flow of ideas and information, which eventually led to the birth of the possibility of invading space, building electronic minds, navigating the issue of genetic engineering, and the birth of the Internet and communications, which created a radical change in people's lives, production and market handling, and building authority and power.

The issue of control and hegemony is disappearing, and the issue of economic and technological capabilities is growing

Building power and authority in the modern era has not become dependent only on blocs and alliances that seek to impose control and hegemony, as was the case in the past, by resorting to force or waving it through the stick of military force that has a high material and human cost.

Rather, the polarity of power has become at present the title of an extended network of social, economic, political, and technological interactions within the international community, that network is based mainly on the elements of the free capitalist system that is currently led by the United States of America and its partners from the countries of Western Europe and Japan.

This leads us to identify the most prominent current networks of power and control in the international community, which are represented by the World Bank, the European Union, the International Monetary Fund, the

International Energy Agency, the World Trade Organization, and the Organization for Economic Cooperation and Development.

Contemporary diplomacy according to the variables of international relations

The general concept of diplomacy refers to it as *"a means of communication and understanding between peoples to work to reconcile the conflicting interests of states, resolve disputes by peaceful means and remove hotbeds of tension, in pursuit of security and peace between peoples and states."*

Contemporary diplomacy applications

Contemporary diplomacy has resulted in many related concepts, such as the multiple diplomacies that are reflected in the diplomacy of organizations, the popular diplomacy that is titled the diplomacy of opinion, and the presidential diplomacy, which is the diplomacy of the summit that is held between the heads and rulers of states and each other.

Different shapes of contemporary diplomacy

Bilateral diplomacy

It is an expression of traditional diplomacy that is based on the principles of communication and negotiation between two countries.

Collective diplomacy

It is the diplomacy of conferences of international or regional organizations or specialized agencies.

Parliamentary diplomacy

It is the diplomacy of the regular sessions of permanent delegations to international parliamentary institutions.

Presidential diplomacy

It is the diplomacy of the summit that comes as a result of the meetings of the leaders of the countries.

Popular diplomacy

It is the diplomacy of communication and direct interaction between people and different political organizations.

Economic diplomacy

It is the diplomacy of economic aid provided by countries bilaterally or collectively.

Objectives of modern activities of contemporary diplomacy

Multi-diplomacy

Engaging in the activities of the United Nations and other specialized international and regional organizations.

Popular diplomacy

This new type of diplomacy works to achieve collective civilizational security, and support deeper relations, especially with popular organizations in other countries.

It also supports human rights movements, encourages the exchange of visits to sports and artistic teams, and establishes relations of cooperation and coordination between student and youth unions in different countries, the same applies to labor unions, writers, artists, and professional, cultural, and religious entities

Presidential diplomacy

This type of contemporary diplomacy is concerned with presidents addressing other people directly, expressing the aspirations of their people toward knowing and cooperating with others in different countries.

Objectives of modern activities of contemporary diplomacy

Comprehensive diplomacy

Go beyond routine work and protocol manifestations, and move towards managing and dealing with issues of international dimensions.

Conference's diplomacy

Holding conferences with specific business schedules to manage and deal with issues of common international concern.

Linkage diplomacy

Formation of regional and international groups with political, economic, and social dimensions.

The role of the United Nations in unifying the foundations of the international diplomatic system

Over the past decade, the United Nations has played a radical role in unifying the foundations of the international diplomatic system, by establishing the basic rules for this system, and working to codify and regulate the rules of diplomatic work, as the most prominent of these roles were:

*- Formulation of rights and privileges based on unified, specific, and agreed-upon legal rules.

*- The Convention on the Immunities and Privileges of United Nations Personnel - 1947.

*- Convention on the Immunities and Privileges of the Specialized Agencies of the United Nations - 1947.

*- Vienna Convention on Diplomatic Relations - 1961.

*- Vienna Convention on Consular Relations - 1963.

*- Vienna Convention on Special Diplomatic Missions - 1969.

*- The Vienna Convention on the Representation of States and Their Relations with International Organizations of a Global Character - 1975.

Models for areas of comprehensive diplomatic activities

*- Holding scientific, cultural, and artistic seminars.

*- Mutual visits for all activities of common interest.

*- Participation in local, regional, and international events.

*- Preparation of bilateral and regional agreements and treaties.

*- Holding workshops to discuss some issues of common interest.

*- Mutual visits of delegations of specialists in various fields of cooperation.

*- Holding scientific and cultural exhibitions and artistic and musical concerts.

Models for conference diplomacy titles

*- Combating illegal immigration.

*- Human rights, children, and women.

*- Reducing the spread of weapons of mass destruction.

*- Combating environmental pollution, diseases, and epidemics.

*- Population and comprehensive and sustainable development.

*- Education, unemployment, and alternative opportunities for work.

*- Combating violence, organized crime, and international terrorism.

Models for regional and international groups

*- European Union.

*- The African Union.

*- Arab Maghreb Union.

*- League of Arab States.

*- Southern African group.

*- GCC. *- The West African Group.

*- The Association of Southeast Asian Nations (ASEAN).

*- The North American Group of Free Trade Agreement (NAFTA).

*- The Southern Common Market group of countries (MERCOSUR).

Challenges of the New World Order

New diplomatic burdens to meet the challenges

Although the new world order has added a new taste to political life worldwide, its main umbrella is cooperation and coordination among countries for the welfare of people, the path of this cooperation and coordination was not strewn with roses as some think, as this system has produced many challenges that It added burdens to the work of the diplomat that was not expected, as some might think, among these challenges is a reconsideration of the organization of the structures and priorities of the various diplomatic departments in the countries in order to confront issues related to contemporary changes that require a new culture and good formation.

These challenges pushed multilateral diplomacy towards working to provide the means to manage the effects of conflicts and civil wars with a tribal, religious, or sectarian dimension, as well as other disputes that may arise as a result of economic crises, corruption, famines, or disasters.

Also, reformulating the various media industry with the message of multilateral diplomacy, considering that the media is one of the most important means of guiding and persuading public opinion on the one hand, when it is supportive of solutions that are difficult to accept, and on the other hand, it is considered one of the things that restrict the work of the diplomatic negotiator in a way that does not allow him bypassing his mission.

The official diplomatic structure of the state

From the point of view of diplomacy, the official diplomatic structural structure of the state is divided into two branches, the first branch of the structure falls under the umbrella of the activities of the so-called **Basic Diplomacy** and this structure includes the head of state (or the king, or the ruler), the minister of foreign affairs, and the permanent diplomatic missions abroad of the state.

As for the so-called **Supporting Diplomacy**, the special diplomatic missions, special missions to international organizations, and diplomacy of regional and international conferences fall under their activities.

These two diplomacies are the tools for implementing the country's foreign policy.

The vocabulary of the official state structure

Powers and controls for granting authority

Chief of the state

The most important powers include attending regional and international conferences, sending and receiving members of the diplomatic corps, declaring war and concluding peace treaties, concluding and ratifying international treaties, exchanging official visits with state leaders, and receiving international officials.

The internal and external powers and authorities of the head of state are subject to his legal status based on several privileges and immunities guaranteed to him by the constitution emanating from the country's political system.

The limits of authority and powers granted to the head of state in the fields of diplomatic and international relations are divided into two types, and the authority and powers of heads of state in the different countries are not the same.

The controls for granting authority and powers to the head of state refer to the existence of the legislative authority (parliament) oversight over the actions of the executive authority (the head of state).

As for the controls for granting authorities and powers about ministerial responsibility, this is due to the responsibility of the Council of Ministers or ministers, to confront the parliament.

Speaking about the privileges and immunities enjoyed by the head of state, we will find that the place where the visiting head of state residents and the place where his accompanying persons reside has immunity against the authorities of the host country, as this country's authorities or officials does not have the power to enter these places without his permission.

The head of state in person, officially visiting another country and delegation accompanying him, also enjoys all the prescribed privileges, as well as personal, civil, and penal immunity in the face of the territorial jurisdiction of the host country, whose principles and rules are derived from public international law.

The purpose of providing privileges and immunities is to facilitate the visit, and respect and uphold the sovereignty of the visiting president's country, whereby he must respect the laws and traditions of the host country, and refrain from doing any act that may offend it, otherwise the host country has the authority to ask him to leave the country and reserves the right to take some specific measures to prevent the recurrence of such acts, provided that the immunities of the visiting head of state and the privileges established and granted to him are not violated.

Controls for granting authority and powers in the monarchy system (example)

Article 33 of the Jordanian constitution states that *"the king is the one who declares war, concludes peace, and concludes treaties and agreements."*.

Controls for granting authority and powers in the republican system (examples)

The Italian president does not have the right to ratify international treaties without the participation of ministers and the approval of Parliament by a law issued for this purpose.

The French President, according to the Constitution of the Fifth Republic, has the powers to conclude international treaties, except for some of them, which must be preceded by the approval of Parliament by a law issued for this purpose.

Minister of Foreign Affairs

The functional concept of the Minister of Foreign Affairs indicates that he is an official employee of the state specializing in managing its foreign relations, and he is also one of the basic and active elements of diplomatic relations, but he often does not enjoy the powers of the supreme authority in his country (such as the president), and he has an important and influential role through his active participation in regional and international conferences and meetings, the scope of his profession's powers vary according to the country's political systems.

The scope and nature of the tasks entrusted to the post of Minister of Foreign Affairs are divided into two types, *internal tasks* represented in heading and managing the Ministry of Foreign Affairs and supervising the country's diplomatic missions abroad, and contributing to the development and implementation of the country's foreign policy through communication with foreign diplomatic missions accredited to the country.

As for the *external tasks*, they are limited to receiving foreign diplomats for consultation and discussion, participating in the conclusion of agreements and treaties and supervising them, attending conferences as a state representative, and traveling on official missions as envoy by the President.

Determining the tasks and competencies of the Minister of Foreign Affairs is one of the internal affairs of states, as it depends on the nature of the country's political system.

The nature of main tasks of the position of the Minister of Foreign Affairs focuses on supervising the preparation and editing of all official documents related to the management of the country's foreign affairs, participating in drafting treaties, agreements, and related protocols, and receiving foreign delegations and personalities are coming to visit the country, participating in the preparation of the various conferences that will be held in the country, representing his country in regional and international conferences and organizations, and conducting discussions with representatives of other countries regarding issues of common concern.

Among his main tasks is to supervise the movement of appointments and transfers to the diplomatic corps in his country, as well as discuss and submit proposals for the appointment of diplomats and consuls on missions from his country to other countries, and coordinate the activity of the various diplomatic missions accredited to his country abroad and receive reports from them.

He must also receive envoys from the foreign diplomatic corps, present them to the head of state, negotiate and talk with them, enable them to perform their duties, supervise the system of their immunities and protect them.

Whoever rises to the position of Minister of Foreign Affairs must follow up on the international situation by collecting information and investigating it through his country's diplomatic missions to others, and submit reports on these situations in a way that benefits his government towards decision-making.

The Minister of Foreign Affairs must work to protect the interests of his country at its various levels, political, economic, commercial, and cultural, and protect his country's nationals and their interests, residents or visitors to foreign countries, through his country's diplomatic or consular missions accredited to these countries, and supervising the proper implementation and sponsorship of treaties concluded with other countries.

The Minister of Foreign Affairs enjoys during his official visits to other countries, and in his capacity as Vice-President and representative of the state, the same legal position established for the head of state in terms of the established privileges and immunities, whose principles and rules are derived from public international law, provided that they do not extend to the minister's visits of a personal nature.

Permanent diplomatic missions of the country

In order to know how the permanent diplomatic missions of countries are born, we must follow the sources of the provisions regulating them and their hierarchy, which began through the provisions of international treaties and agreements, then resorting to recognized, agreed upon, and stable international norms, and going back to the provisions of national laws and judicial rulings.

International treaties and agreements

*- Vienna Regulations for the year 1815.

*- Protocol of Aix-la-Chapelle of 1818.

*- Havana Convention of 1928.

*- Vienna Convention on Diplomatic Relations of 1961.

Vienna Convention on Diplomatic Relations of 1961

An international agreement was reached under the supervision of the United Nations to codify the international norms in force between countries with regard to permanent diplomatic relations, and it is considered the model and the basis for subsequent diplomatic agreements.

One of the most important principles of the Vienna Convention on Diplomatic Relations of 1961 is the integration of conventional and customary legal rules regulating relations between states and diplomatic exchange between them.

And that the diplomatic envoy derives his authority and Immunity from the country he represents and not from the person of the head of state as it was in the past, which justifies the representative capacity of the diplomatic mission.

Diplomatic immunities and privileges must be linked to the requirements of the diplomatic post, and these privileges are granted to diplomatic missions for the purpose of enabling them to carry out their tasks and burdens.

International customaries

These are the tools and behaviors that countries have repeatedly resorted to and compulsorily act on with regard to all matters related to diplomatic representation among them.

Diplomatic customaries are among the unwritten regulatory sources, and they are resorted to by non-signatory states to the Vienna Convention on Diplomatic Relations of 1961., or by the signatory states to this agreement and other non-signatory states.

One of the most important features of international customaries is that it works to fill the gap towards the impossibility of finding the required legal provision in the international agreements of diplomatic law, that is, it is considered a haven to find out the required legal ruling, and to emphasize the importance of international norms.

The Vienna Convention of 1961 stipulated in its preamble that: "The rules of customary international law must continue to be applied to matters not expressly dealt with in the provisions of this convention".

Norms are also a source for defining and regulating the rules of permanent diplomatic exchange adopted by the states parties that are not signatories to bilateral or collective international agreements related to permanent diplomatic law, or that have not been able to provide any internal legislation.

National laws

National legislation may grant diplomatic missions a legal status greater than what is granted to them by international law, but it may not grant them a lower status than that decided by international law in their favor, with regard to matters not included in the internal jurisdiction of the countries.

The national legislation related to the exchange of diplomatic relations comes mostly to meet the requirements of international diplomatic law and its conventions and customary rules, but the national legislation must be harmonious and conform to the provisions and rules of international diplomatic law.

Judicial rulings

The rulings of international and national courts are exceptional sources, and they are considered backup provisions for the rules of international diplomatic law, as they are not among the original sources of diplomatic law, therefore, it is not obligatory for the judge to refer to them to decide the dispute before him, but the judge can refer to them of his own free will and choice. In order to explain the ambiguity of a legal text or in order to stand on an issue.

Conditions for accepting permanent diplomatic exchange between countries

In order to achieve permanent diplomatic exchange between countries, two basic conditions must be met, the first condition refers to **the necessity of international recognition of the state**, which is a prerequisite for the establishment of a permanent diplomatic exchange, it also states that a new social being now enjoys the description of the state and has become eligible to establish legal relations with it.

The second condition is **the availability of the right to diplomatic representation**, as this right is generated based on the established principle in international law according to which **"every independent country that enjoys full** *sovereignty over its territory has the right to international representation."*

Organizational structure of permanent diplomatic missions

The organizational structure of diplomatic missions includes each of its employees, and the various departments, the staff is the diplomatic envoys, administrators, technicians, and employees, and the relevant departments of the mission include the diplomatic attaché, the consular attaché, the commercial attaché, the cultural attaché, the educational attaché, and the defense attaché.

Diplomatic envoys

It is the category of staff in the diplomatic mission that enjoys a political status, and it includes the head of the mission and other members who hold the diplomatic status, the appointment of diplomats is absolutely subject to the authority of his country, which is based on its internal laws that determine the mechanism, manner, and conditions of appointment, provided that this is done while it is consistent with the rules of diplomatic law and its provisions in force among the countries of the world.

The state selection mechanism of heads of diplomatic missions

The nomination comes from the Minister of Foreign Affairs, and then the selection is usually made by the head of the state.

The mechanism for accepting the accreditation of heads of missions to host countries

It is obligatory for the country to be accredited to submit a request to obtain the approval of the host country regarding the appointment of the head of the mission before dispatching him, followed by activating what is called the period of revision from the host country after receiving the request, that period that is allocated for research and investigation.

The host country is not obligated for accepting any envoy or diplomatic representative to head the mission if it does not agree to him without giving reasons, and the reasons for refusal may be due to personal behavior, or for political or ideological reasons, or the envoy is of dual nationality, as most countries stress on that...etc.

The procedures for the arrival of the head of the mission

The procedures for the arrival of the head of the diplomatic mission for the start of his job duties begin with receiving the approval of the appointment from the host country and specifying the arrival time from his country, then informing the concerned mission about the reception ceremony for the head of the mission at the airport, seaport or at the border, after that the double formal notification is made to each of the accrediting country and the host country for the actual arrival.

After the arrival of the head of the mission, a copy of the letter of credential is presented to the Minister of Foreign Affairs of the country to which the diplomatic mission is accredited, after which a date is set for submitting the official letter of credential to the head of the state accredited to it through specific ceremonies, and after completing that, the head of the mission must inform his country in writing officially, by presenting the letter of credential to the head of the host country, marking the start of his duties, and also informing the dean of the diplomatic corps in the host country and other diplomatic missions in writing about the start of his duties.

The level of diplomatic representation and its importance

Diplomatic representation at the embassy level

It is headed by an ambassador, who is in the highest position or rank in a diplomatic mission.

Diplomatic representation at the commission level

It is headed by a minister plenipotentiary who is lower in rank than the ambassador.

Each of the ambassadors and extraordinary representatives of heads of state enjoys the exclusive capacity of representing the president before the head of the host country, and the heads of diplomatic missions do not distinguish between them on the basis of rank or category except with regard to the priority of attendance and presence in the events specified by the protocol.

Categories of other workers in diplomatic missions

Administrators and Technicians

They are the mission staff who are assigned to carry out administrative and technical affairs, such as accounts, archives, communications, secretarial, and personnel affairs.

Services staff

They are assigned to serve the mission, such as cleaning, guarding, and driving cars, while the private servants are not among the employees of the mission but rather among the employees of its members.

The size of the diplomatic mission in the host country

What is meant by the size of the diplomatic mission is the number of personnel working for it, as well as the number of its departments, attachments, or affiliated agencies. The Vienna Convention on Diplomatic Relations of 1961 was approved and specified in its Article No. (11), the details of the criteria that must be relied upon by accredited countries when determining the size of their mission in the host countries.

The size of the diplomatic mission according to the criteria of Article (11) of the Vienna Convention

The principle is the agreement of the accrediting country and the accredited country (the host) on the size of the mission. If there is no agreement between them, the accrediting country may make the size of its mission within the reasonable and usual limits according to what it estimates in view of the circumstances and conditions prevailing in the host country and the needs of the special mission. Knowing that the host country has the right to refuse or to accept employees of a certain category within the same limits referred to above, provided that there is no discrimination regarding this issue.

The activation of the principle of reciprocity is important and has to be considered in this issue

The location of the diplomatic mission in the host country

What has been established by the prevailing diplomatic custom is that the headquarters of the diplomatic mission of the accrediting country be in the capital of the host country, however, Article No. (12) of the Vienna Convention on Diplomatic Relations of 1961 permitted the accrediting country to establish offices for it in cities other than the capital of the host country if the latter expresses its understanding and satisfaction with this matter, that is, the establishment of these offices in other cities within the territory of the host country is subject to its approval and satisfaction.

The activation of the principle of reciprocity is important and has to be considered in this issue

The main functions of permanent diplomatic missions

The main tasks of the permanent diplomatic missions vary between diplomatic jobs, diplomatic representation, protecting the interests of the accredited country in the host country, monitoring and exploring the internal conditions of the host country, managing the accredited country's negotiations with the host country's government, strengthening bilateral relations in various fields and supporting International cooperation, sponsoring citizens of the accredited country who are residents or visitors to the host country.

The permanent diplomatic missions are also looking forward to carrying out consular tasks and works that are of a technical and administrative nature.

Diplomatic Representation

Since the diplomatic mission is a general facility for the accredited country to the host country, the task of diplomatic representation comes at the top of the jobs, and the diplomatic envoys are like messengers or agents for their country and work for it in order to convey its point of view and the tracks of its various policies and the conclusion of treaties and agreements, and preserving its interests and the interests of its nationals in the country that accredits it.

Among these tasks is the conclusion of treaties and agreements, which may be seen by the head of the mission (the ambassador or the chargé d'affaires), who is legally authorized under the Vienna Convention of 1969 on the Law of Diplomatic Treaties, or that a diplomatic envoy rather than the ambassador may be informed to carry out this task, in the presence of a letter of credential to him to get this done.

Protecting the interests of the accredited country in the host country

The ways to protect the interests of the accredited country by the host country are divided into two types, the first type is called *functional diplomatic protection*, which is the protection that is provided to the accredited and permanent diplomatic mission of the accredited country, and the other type of protection is what is called *delegated diplomatic protection*, which works to provide protection for the diplomatic mission that takes care of the other country's interests when it does not have a permanent diplomatic mission in the host country.

Functional diplomatic protection

It is one of the exclusive rights of the accrediting country with the host country based on respect for the rules of international law, and it is a tool to protect the citizens of the accrediting country and compensate them for any damages that may arise for them, but by following certain rules and conditions:

*- The aggrieved party must have the nationality of the accredited country.

*- Exhaustion of the local appeal methods available to the victim in the country to which the mission is accredited.

*- The aggrieved party's failure to contribute to an internationally illegal act that causes harm to the country to which the mission is accredited.

Delegated diplomatic protection

This type of protection is based on the legal relationship that exists between three parties, the country that sponsors the interests, the beneficiary country that was accredited, and the country that is the host, where one of its most important functions is to protect the nationals, their money, their property, and the public property of the beneficiary country by the sponsoring country for the interests of the accredited country, especially when a conflict or war breaks out between the "previously accredited" beneficiary country and the host country.

Monitoring and surveying the internal situation of the host country

It is one of the oldest and most difficult tasks ever, and it is considered highly sensitive and takes two contradictory forms. The first form is good, and it is the one that is stable in international law in both the conventional and customary parts, which require that monitoring and reconnaissance be done by following legitimate methods and means.

The bad form is done through proceeding illegal means, and foremost among them are espionage operations of all kinds, which contributed to a large extent to creating problems and conflicts between countries.

Managing the accredited country's negotiations with the government of the host country

There are two permanent bases for the negotiations that take place between the accrediting country and the host country. The first base refers to the convergence of points of view between the two countries, and the second base is the settlement of existing disputes between the two countries, or the avoidance of any disputes that may occur in the future.

Article 33/1 of the Charter of the United Nations states that "the parties to any dispute, the continuation of which is likely to endanger the maintenance of international peace and security, must, first of all, seek a solution to it through negotiation, investigation, mediation, conciliation, arbitration, judicial settlement, or they may resort to regional agencies and organizations or other peaceful means of their choice.

Features of a successful negotiation environment

It must be known to the missions of the negotiating countries that they are not obligated to reach a certain outcome or an agreement of a certain kind through the stages of negotiation, but rather they have a responsibility and obligation to provide whatever necessary, all useful information and mechanisms that serve these negotiations, and none of the parties should show intransigence or throws obstacles in the course of these negotiations, which may hinder the decision-maker from reaching a solution or agreement.

Managing the accredited country's negotiations with the government of the host country

The management of the negotiation process on issues related to the government of the host country must be carried out through modern mechanisms that have a good outcome, with setting priorities.

The diplomatic mission always has priority in the negotiation process of political significance, and also with regard to political crises.

Technicians and experts are entrusted with the negotiation process related to complex and technical issues, and special missions are entrusted with negotiation processes that include some important and vital issues.

Strengthening bilateral relations and supporting international cooperation

Realistic diplomatic action must always seek to strengthen bilateral relations between the two countries and support the issue of international cooperation with regard to the interest of both parties, and this will only come about by activating the principle of respecting the sovereignty of states, equality in dealing, and non-use of force.

Therefore, permanent diplomatic missions play an important role in mitigating tension, and also adopt the development of bonds of cooperation in various fields, support international cooperation in order to resolve disputes, and participate in international initiatives that target the common interest of the peoples of the world.

Consular functions of permanent diplomatic missions

There are many consular tasks for permanent diplomatic missions, among these tasks are issuing documents, different types of visas, and providing support to nationals, Article No. (5) of the Vienna Convention on Consular Relations of 1963 clarified the tasks assigned to consular missions of countries to include the following:

*- Issuing passports, traveling documents, and the necessary documents for citizens of the accredited country.

*- Issuing different types of visas and necessary documents for those wishing to travel to the approved country.

*- Providing assistance to the its nationals, whether they are normal persons or those who have been convicted.

Representing the nationals before third parties, translation and documentation work

Carrying out translation and documentation works (notaries public), and matters related to the civil status of nationals and foreigners, provided that this is done without contradicting the local laws of the host country and protecting the interests of the citizens of its country with regard to inheritance and legacies, and they provide protection of minors and the incompetent with regard to the imposition of guardianship or interdiction provided that this is done without contradicting the local laws of the host country.

Also, representing their nationals in front of the courts and authorities of the host country, taking the necessary measures to ensure the appropriate representation of these nationals in front of those bodies, and submitting a request to take provisional measures in their favor without prejudice to the laws of the host country.

Dealing with judicial papers and the exercise of the right to control and inspection

Dealing with judicial and non-judicial papers and making representations in accordance with applicable international agreements, or in a manner consistent with the local laws applied in the host country.

Exercising the control and inspection rights stipulated in the laws of the host country on the ships that bear the mission nationality, on the planes registered with it, and on the crews working on those ships and planes.

Providing assistance to the ships and planes belonging to their country and their crews working on them, obtaining statements about the travels of its ships and planes, checking and marking their documents, investigating emergency events, and intervening to settle disputes within the limits permitted by the laws of the host country.

Developing bilateral relations and protecting nationals and interests

Contributing to the development of economic, commercial, cultural, and scientific relations between the two countries, inquiring through legitimate means about the economic, commercial, cultural, and scientific conditions in the host country, and sending reports thereon to their country.

Exercise of any other work assigned to the consular mission by its country to protect its interests and nationals, without prejudice to the prohibition stipulated by the law in the host country or the clear objection from it, or what contradicts has been mentioned in the international agreements or treaties in force in the two signatory countries.

Controls and conditions for the integration of diplomatic missions and consular functions

Article No. (3) of the Vienna Convention on Consular Relations of 1963 permitted diplomatic missions to exercise consular functions, as stipulated by Article No. (2/3) of the Vienna Convention on Diplomatic Relations of 1961, that the provisions of this agreement may not be interpreted in a way that prevents the exercise of the diplomatic mission for consular functions.

Article No. (1/17) of the Consular Relations Agreement of 1963 stipulates that the consular officer can exercise diplomatic functions after the approval of the host country, provided that the accrediting country does not have representation in the host country, either through a diplomatic mission or through a diplomatic mission of a third country.

Reasons for termination of diplomatic missions

There are various reasons leading to the termination of diplomatic missions and the work of the permanent mission in the host country, which comes as a result of the severance of diplomatic relations between the two countries, the demise of the right to diplomatic representation, non-recognition of unconstitutional governments of states, the termination of diplomatic representation for non-political reasons, or the suspension of diplomatic relations. and freeze mission activity.

Severing diplomatic relations

Severing diplomatic relations is considered a unilateral act by one of the countries, as it comes as an expression of its will towards putting a final end to its channels of communication with another country/countries, which often happens due to the deterioration arising in the tracks of the existing relations between them.

This severance may come as a prelude or a warning of the outbreak of war between them, and it should be noted that the decision to sever diplomatic relations is not taken randomly or emotionally, but rather it must be based on fundamental reasons that justify taking such a decision because of its negative effects on both sides.

The reasons for severing diplomatic relations are either ***procedural reasons, or legal reasons***, generated as a result of a violation of the principles on which it is based and adopted by an international organization by one or more of its member countries, or a violation by one of the countries of the obligation that falls upon it under international law, such as the interference of the accredited country in the affairs of the host country or vice versa, or the host country's abuse of the citizens of the accredited country.

The effects of severing diplomatic relations

Among the consequences of severing diplomatic relations between countries is the closure of the permanent diplomatic mission, the withdrawal of its members from the host country, and the obligation of the host country to protect the headquarters of the closed mission and its assets, records, and funds.

The host country also has the right to entrust a third country approved by the country that has the closed mission so that this third country becomes a country that sponsors its interests in the host country.

Severing diplomatic relations between two countries do not affect their right to establish and send special diplomatic missions between them, the purpose of which is consultation and discussion on specific issues of common interest to both countries.

Among the effects also is facilitating the stay of the members of the closed mission while preserving the privileges and immunities granted to them until they leave the territory of the host country based on the provisions of Article No. 39/2 of the Vienna Convention on Diplomatic Relations of 1961.

Also, the severance of diplomatic relations between countries that are signatories to international treaties does not affect the obligations of those countries towards these treaties and their membership in them, unless there is an indication in the terms of those treaties to the inevitability of the availability of diplomatic relations, which results in the impossibility of continuing with these treaties as a result of severing diplomatic relations.

Losing the right to diplomatic representation

The disappearance of the international legal personality of a country (host or accredited to it), as a result of its dissolution or union with another country to create a new state, or because it is subject to international protection or occupation, all of which becomes a major reason for ending the representation of its permanent diplomatic mission.

Non-recognition of unconstitutional governments of states

The non-recognition of the unconstitutional governments of the host countries or the countries accredited to them is considered a direct reason for either severing relations when the new government is not recognized or suspended between countries, given that the formation of such governments often comes after the occurrence of coups or revolutions and as a result, the country's rule will be taken over by a group of people in a way other than the decree and specified in the country's constitution that the people asked for a referendum.

The severance of relations comes as a sign of non-recognition of the new government, and the suspension of relations is taken until the situation is settled and the new government is recognized, as then and due to that new diplomatic credentials must be submitted.

The suspension of diplomatic relations between the two countries, that is, the temporary freezing of the activities of the permanent diplomatic mission, do not put a final end to the existing diplomatic relations between the two countries, as this activity is restored once the reason leading to this suspension has disappeared, and the return of this activity is not followed by resorting to a new agreement between the two countries.

Suspension of diplomatic relations between countries for an indefinite period

Among the forms of suspending diplomatic relations between countries is summoning the head of the mission, which will have a significant impact on the mission's activity due to the reduction of its basic tasks towards representation and negotiation, or summoning the members of the mission (all or some of them), and the impact of this is limited on the mission's activity, and Article No. (45) From the Vienna Convention on Diplomatic Relations of 1961, it did not address the obligation of the accrediting country to provide justifications or reasons for the summons.

Termination of diplomatic representation for non-political reasons

Some countries resort to ending their diplomatic representation due to financial reasons, which entails the closure of the permanent mission and the withdrawal of its members from the host country, and termination in this sense is not considered a final severance of diplomatic relations, as the country with this mission can either transfer the affairs of its diplomatic mission to its permanent consulate, or agreeing to a third country in order to take care of its interests, or resorting to an individual or joint representation of the head of the mission to the host countries stipulated in Articles No. (5) and (6) of the Vienna Convention on Diplomatic Relations of 1961.

The reasons for termination of the duties of the diplomatic envoy

The reasons for resorting to summoning the diplomatic envoy or the termination of his duties in the permanent diplomatic mission range from, the death of the diplomatic envoy, expulsion from the host country, promotion or upgrading to a higher degree, or running for another position inside or outside his country, or for personal reasons related to the diplomatic envoy himself or change the person of the king in countries that enjoy the monarchy, or summon the diplomatic envoy to a town for various reasons, or change the place of work of the diplomatic envoy, or transfer him to another place of work, or the deterioration of the relationship of the diplomatic envoy with the country to which he is accredited as a result of lack of confidence or failure to implement correctly the policy of his government, or his misconduct or disorderly conduct in the host country.

Expulsion from the host country

Procedures for terminating the duties of the head of the mission or one of the unwanted diplomats, administrators, technicians, or employees are carried out by informing the concerned diplomatic mission officially of the name of the unwanted person on the territory of the host country, giving him an appropriate period to leave the country.

In the event that the person whose presence in the country is not wanted does not comply with the request of the host country, or is not summoned by his country after the expiration of the period granted to him to leave, the host country has the right to arrest and deport him to the airport, seaport or border to expel him from the country.

Promotion or upgrading of a diplomatic envoy to a higher level

The diplomatic duties of the envoy are considered terminated in the host country if he is promoted or upgraded to the rank of Chargé d'affaires, Minister Plenipotentiary, or to the rank of Ambassador, and he continues to remain in that host country in which he was working under his previous rank, then he must submit a new letter of accreditation including his diplomatic rank that he submits it to the government of the host country.

Changing the personality of the king in countries that enjoy the monarchy

Countries that enjoy a monarchy consider that diplomatic representation is tantamount to a personal representation of the king of the country, so if this king is changed in person, the previous accreditation of the diplomatic envoy (head of the mission) has expired, and the envoy has to submit a new letter of credential in his favor with the signature of the new king to the government of the host country, this is not the case in countries that enjoy republican systems.

Personal reasons related to the diplomatic envoy

The personal reasons related to the diplomatic envoy that led to the termination of his duties in the permanent diplomatic mission vary between resignation, retirement, crippling illness, or death, and these reasons together are linked to the laws and regulations of the accredited country and have nothing to do with the host country.

Provided that the diplomatic envoy continues to enjoy the privileges and immunities granted to him under international law until his departure from the host country, and in the event of death, the same applies to his family members for a reasonable period of time to manage their affairs, until they are able to leave the host country.

The responsibility of the diplomatic mission for the excesses of its envoys

When a diplomatic envoy exceeds the limits of his powers or undertakes an act that he is not authorized to do by his country, his country does not absolve him of responsibility for his actions, given that the diplomatic mission is a facility of the accredited country and recognized by the host country, and if the accredited country is represented To the host country through a third diplomatic mission (a mission that sponsors its interests), based on Article No. (45) / b and c, and Article No. (46) of the Vienna Convention on Diplomatic Relations of 1961, the responsibility, in this case, will lie with the sponsoring country and not on the accredited country.

Special diplomatic missions

The source of the provisions governing them

The General Assembly of the United Nations Organization approved the Convention on Special Diplomatic Missions in 1969, and defined those special missions in its article (1/a) as *"a temporary mission that represents a country and sends it to another country with the consent of that other country to deal with it with certain issues or to perform a specific task."* This agreement entered into force in 1985.

The motives for its establishment

The motives for establishing special diplomatic missions are due to seek to provide urgent solutions to a problem or a dispute or to carry out tasks that are not desirable to be carried out through permanent diplomatic or consular missions, or to resort to negotiation with people in the host country, who have a higher level than what is available, i.e. their rank higher of the members of the permanent diplomatic mission, or that the subject of negotiation requires persons with special knowledge and who are scientifically or technically qualified.

The most important features

The tasks and functions of the special diplomatic mission are determined and agreed upon by mutual agreement with the host country, according to what was stated in Article No. (3) of the agreement, where the dispatch of the special diplomatic mission between countries is not dependent on the presence or absence of permanent diplomatic or consular representation, according to what was stated in Article No. (7) of the Special Diplomatic Missions Agreement of 1969.

A country may also dispatch a special and joint mission to two or more host countries, and two or more countries may also dispatch a special mission to deal with a matter of common importance, and in both cases, the approval and consent of the host country must be obtained.

The mission may consist of members of permanent and accredited diplomatic or consular missions, in which case these members retain their diplomatic or consular privileges and immunity, and at the same time acquire the privileges and immunities prescribed for the special missions.

The tasks and functions of the special missions are terminated according to the agreement of the sending and host countries on the period required for the work of the mission, and the severing of diplomatic or consular relations between the two countries does not lead to the termination of the work of the special missions that existed before the severance occurred, because their presence in the first place was not linked or dependent on the establishment of diplomatic or consular relations between the two countries.

Dealing with parties within the host country

This type of diplomatic mission must deal with the official authorities through the Ministry of Foreign Affairs of the host country, meaning that the Ministry of Foreign Affairs is the bridge on which the requests of the special diplomatic mission, are addressed to any official body in the host country.

As for the issue of dealing with unofficial bodies in the host country, the basis of Article No. (22) of the Special Diplomatic Missions Agreement obliges the host country to provide the necessary facilities for the mission to carry out its tasks and functions, as among these facilities is entering into informal relations with non-governmental bodies and agencies within the host country, but with respect to the restrictions stipulated in Article No. (47) of the agreement, which refers to the obligation to respect the laws of the host country and not to interfere in its internal affairs.

Immunities and privileges

Special diplomatic missions enjoy two types of immunity in the host country, namely the immunity of the mission's headquarters, and the immunity and privileges of the staff, with the knowledge that the immunity of the special mission's headquarters is relative and not absolute, like what is provided to the accredited and permanent diplomatic missions, and staff in special missions enjoy the same privileges and immunities established for permanent diplomatic missions, however, there are some minor differences with regard to civil judicial immunity.

Article No. (25) of the Special Diplomatic Missions Agreement states that *"the sanctity of the premises in which the special mission resides is safeguarded, so that it is not permitted to enter it except with the consent of the head of the mission and, when necessary, with the consent of the head of the permanent diplomatic mission of the sending country accredited to the host country, and if it is not possible to obtain that approval. The consent to*

enter the headquarters of the special mission is assumed in cases of extreme necessity, such as the occurrence of a fire or an accident that seriously threatens public safety."

Article No. (31/2/d) of the Special Diplomatic Missions Agreement excludes state representatives in the dispatched special mission from civil jurisdiction in the courts of the host country and in the case of lawsuits related to compensation for damages that may arise from the mission's vehicle accidents when they are used abroad the official scope of work by the concerned or related person.

Termination of the special diplomatic mission's job

Among the reasons for the termination of the work of non-permanent (special) diplomatic missions is the termination of the job of the mission and recalling to its country or the achievement of the purpose for which it was established.

Special missions accredited
to int. organizations

The special missions accredited to international and regional organizations have become playing an important role in managing the foreign relations of states, due to the multiplicity of parties who represent members of the organization from the participating missions, which allows for greater flexibility and speed in communication, and has also come to reflect another distinction as it is a kind of institutional diplomacy and not relational like the existing one between countries and each other as permanent diplomatic missions.

One of the most important features of this type of mission indicates that international and regional organizations have the authority to set their own rules regarding the establishment of permanent missions to them, and any member state of an international or regional organization can establish a permanent mission for it if the rules in force within the organization allow it, and it is considered. The agreements to determine the headquarters of the international or regional organization in one of the countries are among the rules regulating its work and among the articles of its internal law.

The permanent mission accredited to international organizations is based on a relationship that combines three parties: the accredited state, the relevant international or regional organization, and the host country of that organization, which nullifies the rights of the principle of reciprocity between the accredited country and the host country.

The international or regional organizations do not enjoy sovereignty and do not have a specific territory to exercise, it has a regional legal jurisdiction that expresses itself through permanent bodies that include international employees or representatives of its member states, hosted by one of the countries.

The tasks and functions of the special missions accredited to the international organizations

The Convention on the Representation of Countries Accredited to International Organizations of 1975 defined the tasks and functions of permanent diplomatic missions accredited to them, which include ensuring the representation of the accredited country to the relevant organization, maintaining the existing bilateral relations between the accredited country and the concerned organization, and bringing support from the member countries of the organization to achieve its objectives, protecting the interests of the member countries of the concerned organization through existing relations with it, adopting the approach of negotiation between the accredited country and the concerned organization and with the rest of the member countries, and ensuring the participation of the member countries in the activities of the organization and sending reports thereon to their countries.

Controls and conditions for establishing special diplomatic missions accredited to international organizations

The sending country may nominate and appoint one person as the head of a permanent mission to be accredited to more than one international organization, and two or more countries may nominate and appoint one person as the head of a permanent mission for each of them / of them accredited to one of the organizations.

The permanent diplomatic missions accredited to international organizations may be its accreditation terminated as a result of either forced or voluntary closure of the mission, or the demise and liquidation of the international organization, or its transfer to another country.

In case is proven that the establishment of a permanent mission to be accredited to an international or regional organization was contrary to the provisions of the internal law and procedural rules in force in the concerned organization, the host country (the headquarters country) has the right to submit an objection to the CEO of the organization to stop this establishment until the reasons for this objection are removed, or validated.

Article No. (77) of the Convention on the Representation of Countries in International Organizations of 1975 required members of diplomatic missions in these organizations to respect the laws in force in the host country (the headquarters country) and not to interfere in its internal affairs, and in both cases, it is required that the concerned member is inside the scope of the exercise of his duties or his job within the mission.

Immunities and privileges

The inadmissibility of arresting representatives of the member countries accredited to the international organization or seizing their luggage, providing the immunity and the inviolability of their papers and documents is guaranteed, as well as the right to make free communication and correspondence. Members of non-governmental missions, or those classified under the category of observers, whether they are permanent or temporary, also enjoy also by the foregoing immunities and privileges

The provision of security and protection by the host country for the members of the permanent diplomatic missions accredited to the international organizations based on its soil, and the representatives of the member countries of the international organization are not subject to the restrictions on residency and immigration regulations in force in the host country (the headquarters country).

And the member country of the international organization will always be obligated to waive the immunity of any of its representatives accredited to the organization granted by the host country, in cases where it is proven that this immunity stands in the way of achieving justice, or that lifting this immunity from its representatives would not affect the purpose that this immunity was decided for them

Diplomacy of regional and international conferences

Conferences diplomacy is what is relating to the meetings that are held for representatives of countries and international bodies in order to consult and discuss reaching solutions or treatment for issues that attract the attention of these countries depending on the basic relations of their countries with international and regional organizations, the nature and method of work of those organizations so that this type of diplomacy has become one of the modern methods with a deep impact and increasing interaction towards addressing all the challenges and risks facing the peoples of the world.

The types of conferences are divided according to their nature into political, scientific, or technical, and according to the participating parties, bilateral or multilateral, and according to the level of representation, ministerial, or at the level of officials, or summit conferences, or conferences at the expert level.

Summit diplomacy

Summit diplomacy is known as that diplomacy that is managed through conferences held by heads of state and governments of the world, which are called presidential conferences or summit conferences, where the purpose is to quickly reach some political decisions or conclude some agreements or treaties that serve their countries.

There are many types of summit conferences, either according to the timing of their convening, such as regular conferences, emergency conferences, or protocolar conferences, or according to their nature, i.e., local, international, bilateral, or multilateral conferences.

Advantages of summit diplomacy

Among the advantages of the diplomacy of the summit, conferences are the opportunity for heads of state and government to confront each other directly, for acquaintance and understanding in an environment surrounded by freedom of expression and frankness to make crucial decisions.

The opinions of ambassadors and diplomatic envoys play an advisory and supportive role in the orientations of the president or prime minister during the summit, and therefore the accredited diplomatic representation loses some aspects of privileges and precedence, but temporarily, they return to normal situation once the summit works are over.

Modern trends of contemporary diplomacy

The origin of the modern trends of contemporary diplomacy is due to the emergence of the information society, the change towards the foundations of human life, the concepts of the new world order, what has been developed in the system of international relations, and the current reality towards the disappearance of barriers to a large extent between the internal and external policy of states, and between local and regional issues, and between war and peace, and between the state itself and its citizens, and the increase in the influence of modern means of communication, which had the greatest impact on the growing influence on the process of making foreign policies of states and the means of their implementation.

Effects of the development of means of communication on diplomatic work

The effects of the development of the means of communication on diplomatic work were manifested through the speed of human movement from one place to another, the speed of moving things from one place to another (diplomatic pouch bags and shipments), the speed of transmission of ideas, exchange cultures, and events, and the speed of providing services despite the distance.

Reducing the scope of the job and limiting the authority granted to the diplomat

In this era, the diplomat shifted from the degree of the original negotiator to the degree of coordinator for the negotiations of someone higher than him (the foreign minister, or president of the state), and this transformation originated due to the effect of the speed of information transmission on diplomatic work, and the collection of work vocabulary became easier, and the implementation of work vocabulary became more difficult, also the classification and analysis for decision-making have become compatible with the requirements of the speed of the times.

These combined and innovative matters give rise to what we can call immediate diplomacy, which led to the expansion of the common space between all of what is called media diplomacy and official diplomacy, which ultimately led to the ease of rulers and governments' communication with other peoples of other countries.

Diplomacy and development programs in the countries

The foreign policy priorities of countries with emerging economies (developing countries) have become directed toward working to mobilize economic resources, bring investment opportunities, and attract and encourage tourism, therefore, it has become the responsibility of foreign work agencies, i.e. the diplomatic missions, to focus on encouraging exports, attracting investments, and importing the required technology, work to increase trade exchange with other countries, encourage and promote tourism activity, take care of the interests of the country's citizens, and link them to the motherland.

The framework of the rules of the concept of diplomacy for development programs that it works on is providing food and water, the management of energy problems, the treatment of the issue of foreign debt, negotiating the prices of raw materials, and effective participation in the international economic system because the economic groups and blocs play an important role within the framework of development programs.

Diplomacy and national security of the country

There is a difference between the classical concepts of security and the concepts of modern security. The concept of classical security always referred to the protection of the states from external risk, while the modern concept of security refers to securing an appropriate standard of living, with the improvement of living conditions and the assertion of sovereignty over resources by states, and this matter led to a fundamental shift in the context of international interactions, from strategic interactions to economic, cultural and social interactions based on diversity in economic resources and trading partners, focus on performance and the search for larger economic entities that gathering small countries.

Diplomacy, belief and religious dimensions

One of the most prominent features of modern conflicts was the birth of the so-called diplomacy of the century, which has an ethnic, national, and religious character, and one of the most prominent features of this diplomacy was spreading a culture of positive negotiation across different cultures on scientific and ethical grounds, and following a path parallel to the official path in the presence of cooperation between them to achieve just goals, adhere to human values to rationalize behavior, achieve stability and build strength in all fields, establish a serious and effective dialogue between the various religious sects, and employ the common ground to consolidate a just peace and distance from all forms of violent extremism.

Diplomacy and international non-governmental organizations

It is every grouping, association, or movement formed in a viable manner by people belonging to different countries for the purpose of achieving goals that do not include profit, which is towards building various forms of human solidarity that transcend borders in order to create a global civil society that monitors the activities and policies of countries in the fields of human rights.

Humans, the environment, and social and humanitarian issues are of common interest.

Basic features of international non-governmental organizations

*- Comprehensiveness of activities covering various fields and areas.

*- Their numbers increase and multiply as they approach the fifteen thousand barriers globally or more.

*- Gradual spread to the world's continents while retaining its main centers in America and Western Europe.

Advantages of these organizations

*- The apparent influence as an active force within international events and conferences in all their forms.

*- Increasing the ability to penetrate the cultures of people and influence the overall values and concepts.

*- Focusing on the role of the individual in formulating and developing new concepts and his ability to influence the mechanisms of international relations directly.

*- Represents a form of informal diplomatic activity, and contributes to solving global and national problems, establishing peace, and achieving stability in the international community, which makes it a supportive auxiliary to official bilateral and multilateral diplomacy.

Diplomacy and international trade affairs

One of the most important axes of contemporary diplomacy is addressing the differences that arise between countries regarding issues related to foreign trade, and what cannot be overlooked is the mutual influence between diplomacy and international trade.

International trade diplomacy tracks

There are many tracks of what is called international trade diplomacy, between bilateral trade diplomacy between countries, and multilateral trade diplomacy, which is reflected in the activities of regional integration organizations for international trade, and the World Trade Organization.

Here, the reference must be directed to the traditional functions related to international trade, which include setting the legal rules governing international commercial relations, creating the appropriate legal framework and political environment at the regional and international levels, activating dispute settlement mechanisms, and imposing the economic sanctions on the countries to compel them to comply with their obligations and pledges.

Bilateral trade diplomacy between countries

The mutual influence between bilateral diplomacy and trade between countries

Bilateral trade diplomacy between countries is considered an effective way to address disputes related to sustainable development, and an important way to give developing countries the opportunity to participate effectively in the areas of international trade in order to support their development programs, and the ultimate goal is to harmonize the national commercial interests of countries with their foreign policies.

Multilateral international trade diplomacy

World Trade Organization (WTO)

The World Trade Organization is considered the regulatory and institutional reference for international trade diplomacy, as it supervises the application of multilateral international trade agreements, which is the basis of the General Agreement on Tariffs and Trade, and is considered an international treaty whose aim is to liberalize world trade and remove customs and other trade barriers and the barriers set by countries with regard to the flow of goods across borders.

Regional integration organizations for international trade

It is an independent international entity that is established by the agreement of some countries in one of the geographical regions of the world to exercise competencies related to cross-border regional trade routes.

Diplomacy and environmental affairs

Active parties related to environmental affairs

The relevant actors in this regard consist of the countries for participation and providing support, governmental organizations, for designing and establishing environmental protection systems, designing and providing human resources management programs, and non-governmental organizations, for participation and submission of proposals.

Mechanisms of conferences related to environmental affairs

The mechanisms of this type of conference arc limited to arranging for preparatory meetings, preparing agendas, arranging for ministerial negotiations, embodying the ideas and principles to be achieved, preparing the standards that must be met by the country's delegation participating in these conferences, and emphasizing the availability of diplomatic skills among the members of the participating delegation.

Also, the mechanism emphasizes the availability of the necessary experience related to the subject of the conference among the members of the delegation and the active participation in the conference committees and the side work related to it informally.

Updated forms to activate the results of the conferences

Among the new forms emerging from the activation of the recommendations and outcomes of conferences related to environmental affairs are **the official international instruments**, which are binding international framework agreements.

Also, **the informal international instruments**, which reflect principles and guidelines that can be applied urgently to solve environmental problems, compared to framework agreements whose activation may be delayed if countries refrain from signing them, and this type of instrument is not binding.

Diplomacy and human rights affairs

The issue of human rights has become one of the main concerns in international relations and has become a focal point for the diplomatic activities of states within international and regional organizations alike.

Human rights legal obligation and the related international conventions entail legal obligations under the following conditions:

*- The state is a party to this agreement.

*- The agreement is entered into force with the completion of the legal quorum of the members.

*- Work to conclude regional or international agreements related to human rights affairs.

Diplomatic mechanisms for human rights affairs

The mechanisms of human rights diplomacy are divided into two parts: the institutional mechanisms, and the conventional mechanisms, the institutional mechanisms include each of the organs operating within the framework of international organizations, such as the Security Council, the United Nations General Assembly, the Economic and Social Council, and the High Commissioner for Human Rights.

Conventional mechanisms include each of the bodies established through international agreements for oversight, such as investigation and documentation bodies, and judicial bodies (international courts).

Modern diplomacy has become a major contributor towards the formulation of legal rules related to human rights affairs, that is, it has become a semi-legislative diplomacy, which is also concerned with international disputes related to human rights, and therefore it has a quasi-judicial function to settle these disputes.

Consular affairs and practice ... introduction

The beginning of the consular institution in the sense known today in the world of diplomacy goes back to the second half of the Middle Ages, as merchants in the Italian, Spanish, and French commercial cities used to choose one or more of them to play the role of arbitrator in commercial disputes and to protect their interests, especially in the commercial centers that knew many consulates in the East in Beirut, Tripoli, Sidon, and Cyprus.

The consular institution expanded in that era through the system of capitulations, under which western merchants and nationals of European countries became subject to the laws of their countries over the territories under the sultanate of the Ottoman Empire.

According to the system of privileges, including civil and criminal jurisdiction, the powers of the consul's practice over their citizens residing in the territories of the Ottoman Empire, protecting the privileges, life, and property of these citizens, following that, the consular institution was transferred to Western Europe, and the Italian consuls spread to the Netherlands, Sweden, Denmark, Norway, and Italy.

With the advent of the nineteenth century and with the development of trade and navigation, the consular position became more important for states and became an integral part of international life. Therefore, states sought to regulate the functions, privileges, and immunities of consuls through concluding international treaties and agreements. Some states also issued internal laws for this purpose. Great Britain enacted the Consuls Act in 1825. It is noticeable that despite the historical extension of the consular institution, the aspects related to the nature of the functions and immunities of the consuls did not develop in a manner consistent or commensurate with the historical extension, as happened with regard to diplomatic relations.

Countries preferred to resort to bilateral treaties to regulate their consular relations instead of finding general international rules of application in this regard, but the matter was completely different in the middle of the twentieth century, as the International Law Committee of the United Nations prepared an international agreement on consular relations that was adopted in Vienna in 1963 at the conference of the United Nations for Consular Relations.

The aforementioned agreement entered into force in 1967, despite the clear influence of the Vienna Convention on Diplomatic Relations of 1961 on the Vienna Convention on Consular Relations of 1963, however, the latter cannot be described as the former in terms of rationing the rules of customary international law in the field of diplomatic relations.

The Convention on Consular Relations included new rules and introduced provisions that were not known in consular relations, and the agreement was also inspired by many legal provisions stipulated in the 1961 Convention on Diplomatic Relations, this does not seem unusual because the trend in international relations today is the trend towards merging consular services with diplomatic relations.

Contemporary consular relations have become governed by legal rules included in the Vienna Convention on consular relations and the bilateral agreements and treaties that countries concluded in abundance before the Vienna Convention of 1963 in the field of consular relations did not provide much for International Law Commission when it developed the draft convention on consular relations.

Consular relations and regulations

The establishment of consular relations, as in the case of diplomatic relations, is based on the principle of mutual consent, no country may establish a consular post for itself in another country without the consent of the host country, which is confirmed by Article (2/1) of the Consular Relations Agreement, which states that "consular relations can only be established based on mutual agreement between countries", and Article (1/4) added that "the host country must agree to establish a consular post over its territory", but this approval is not required to be expressed implicitly in accordance with the provision of Article (2/2) of the 1963 Convention, in which the agreement to establish diplomatic relations also includes approval to establish consular relations unless the agreement stipulates otherwise.

When states establish consular posts (consulate general, consulate, consular representation, or consular agency), they are often keen to appoint career and honorary consuls at the same time, although some are satisfied with appointing career consuls, it is a classification that is in fact consistent with the classes of consular staff according to the provisions of the 1963 Convention.

Types of states consuls

Career Consul

Vienna Convention on Consular Relations of 1963 did not include a specific definition of the career consul, but the prevailing definition of the career consul is that he is a person appointed by the sending country to practice the consular work specifically in exchange for a salary paid to him for this purpose, so the career consul is working only at the consulate, and shall not perform any other professional activity in the host country outside of his consular functions.

It is clear from the previous definition that the career consul is considered an official employee of the sending country, and he receives a regular salary from his country in accordance with its laws and regulations in force and does not undertake any other paid work other than his consular work inside the host country.

The career consul usually enjoys the nationality of his sending country. Article (22) of the Vienna Convention on Consular Relations decides, in principle, that the consular employee should be a citizen of the sending country, and he may hold the nationality of the host country, provided that the latter agrees, and it may withdraw its approval whenever it wants.

Honorary Consul

Vienna Convention on Consular Relations of 1963 defined the honorary consul, as the case for the career consul. An honorary consul is every person entrusted with carrying out a consular mission without receiving a regular salary from the sending country, and this country allows him to practice acquired activities in the host country.

It is clear from the foregoing that honorary consuls are persons who do not professionalize consular work in the first place, and unlike career consuls, they do not receive regular salaries, and they perform their services free of charge or deduct a certain percentage of the consular revenues that they obtain as a result of their work. Also, they are not public figures or officials, and therefore they are not subject to the conditions of appointment that must be met by career consuls, and countries usually choose them from people who enjoy a prominent social or financial status so that they can perform their duties easily.

It is also not required that the honorary consuls be citizens of the host country or reside on its territory, and if this is the case with regard to the honorary consul, then his appointment, pursuant to the provisions of Article (22) of the Vienna Convention on Consular Relations, which requires obtaining the express and prior approval of the host country if he is carrying the nationality of the host country, or if he holds the nationality of a third country if it decides to retain this right in such a case.

The honorary consul performs a profession other than the consular work in principle. He may be a businessman, trader, contractor, or owner of another profession, and he exercises consular duties in addition to his private work.

It should be noted that a number of specialists and countries also argued that the position of honorary consul has become useless now and that the need and logic call for its abolition, especially since the reality has proven that they care about their own and commercial interests more than they care about the interests of the sending country and the interests of its citizens.

Many countries, including the United States, the former Soviet Union, and Australia, canceled the work of appointing honorary consuls abroad and replaced them with career consuls, also it is noted that the Vienna Convention on Consular Relations of 1963 in Article (68) of it made states free to appoint or accept honorary consuls, this leaves the opportunity for countries wishing to maintain the institution of honorary consuls, especially for economically weak and poor countries that usually resort to appointing honorary consuls in order to avoid financial expenses that they may be unable to meet if they resort to appointing career consuls.

Grades or ranks of consuls

Article (9/1) of the Vienna Convention on Consular Relations made it clear that heads of consular missions are divided into four grades or ranks: consuls general, consuls, deputy consuls, and agents of consuls. This is because it does not restrict the right of any state party to the 1963 Vienna Convention on Consular Relations to assign other grades and designations to consular officers other than heads of consular posts.

Consuls General

Consuls General are usually appointed to head a Consulate General to which several consular districts belong, which means that many consuls report to it, or that it exercises its powers over a very large consular area. It is axiomatic that the Consul General enjoys presidential and supervisory powers over all consular staff working in the consular area or areas under his jurisdiction and powers.

The Consul General is subject to the head of the diplomatic mission, and if the country that sent him did not have a diplomatic mission in the host country, he is directly linked to the Ministry of Foreign Affairs.

Consuls

Consuls are usually appointed to supervise small consular areas or to work in small provinces, cities, or ports that do not require the establishment of a general consular post.

Vice-Consuls

They are assistants to the consul general and to the consuls, and they exercise their powers in their absence, and they may be appointed according to the internal laws in force in some countries, or by the consul general or the consul, provided that the sending country agrees or accepts that. There are some cases in which the vice-consuls are the original heads of small consular posts, which are usually called consular representation because the workload does not require the establishment of a consulate general or a consulate.

Consular Agents

They are agents, but of a consular nature, and are usually appointed by a Consul General or Consul, with the consent of the sending country powers, to exercise definite consular functions in a number of small towns or counties within a given consular district, and the consular agents are not directly subordinate to the sending country, because they are not independent of the consul general or the consul who appointed them, and they are directly responsible to them, and each consul general or consul is responsible for the consular agents in front of his government, and because these consular agents are usually appointed from among the citizens of the host country, a number of concerned people went on to consider them in the category of honorary consuls, and for them, this view is supported by the fact that consular agents may in some cases engage in commercial business outside the scope of their consular duties.

The unclear situation regarding consular agents has left its imprint on the Vienna Convention on Consular Relations. Article (9) as it makes consular agents a category of heads of consular missions, and Article (69) of the same Convention stipulates that each state party to the Convention is free to establish or admission consular agencies managed by consular agents who have not been appointed heads of consular posts by the sending State. Article (69) does not consider consular agents heads of consular missions.

The appointment of consuls

International law does not impose any obligation on countries to accept their consuls. Consular relations are based on mutual consent, and no consular mission can be established without the approval of the host country.

Countries practically accept the establishment of consular missions on their territory, a country that may refuse this fears that it will not be allowed to establish consulates abroad, based on the principle of reciprocity, in return, each country enjoys the right to appoint consuls abroad, after the approval of the host country.

The heads of consular missions are also appointed by the sending country, and they are allowed to carry out their duties by the host country. The appointment and acceptance of the heads of consular missions are subject to the legislation, customs, and regulations in force in both the sending and the host countries.

Acquisition of the status of head of a consular mission is subject to two issues: providing him with the consular patent or the consular authorization letter, by the sending country, and with consular exequatur by the host country.

With regard to the consular patent or the consular authorization letter, the sending country provides it to the head of the consular mission, and it is a document issued in the form of a patent or a document in which the sending country proves the capacity, rank, category, area of competence, and headquarters of the consular mission, as it is an official authorization issued by the sending country to the head of the consular post to perform consular functions on its behalf in the host country.

The consular patent differs from the letter "Accreditation of Heads of Diplomatic Missions in that the former is not addressed to the President of the host State or to its Minister of Foreign Affairs in the case of the appointment of a Chargé d'affaires, as the consular patent is not addressed to a specific person in particular but to whom it may concern" or "to everyone who has access to it, and the consular patent does not precede the host country review the status of the head of the consular post, as is the case in the case of the appointment of heads of diplomatic missions.

Consular patent is sent in accordance with the provisions of Article (11/2) of the Vienna Convention on Consular Relations by diplomatic means. Usually, the sending country sends it to the host country through its diplomatic mission accredited to the latter. If it does not have permanent diplomatic relations, then it is sent through the consular mission of the sending country. If it does not have a consular mission, it is sent by any other means such as mail or through a diplomatic mission to a third country.

If the host country agrees to appoint the head of the consular mission named in the consular patent, it allows him to carry out his duties and functions through what is called a consular exequatur, and the allow is not required.

The consular exequatur does not require a specific form, as it is merely a license issued by the host country that allows the head of the consular mission to perform his consular functions.

It is customary for the consular exequatur to be issued by the executive authority, so the appointment of heads of consular missions, the issuance of consular acquittals, and the granting of consular exequatur are all governed by the internal laws in force in the concerned countries, and they are not subject to single standards and rules, but the issuance of a consular exequatur is usually confined between the head of the country and a minister foreign affairs, and the host country is not obligated to issue consular exequatur, it has the absolute right to refuse to grant consular exequatur without showing the reasons that push it to take this situation.

It is natural that the consular exequatur is not issued immediately upon receipt of the host country, as the latter may require time for its issuance, which necessitates support for the provisions of Article (13) of the Consular Relations Agreement of 1963 to allow the head of the consular mission to begin exercising his functions, and for this reason, the aforementioned article approved the rule of temporary admission of the heads of the host countries, it is not obligated to approve the request of the sending country to obtain temporary admission to the head of its consular post, nor is it obligated to indicate the reasons for the refusal.

The consular mission is not limited to its head, as it consists of the head in addition to a number of consular employees whose appointment does not require following the same procedures for appointing the head of the consular mission.

The Vienna Convention of 1963 appreciates the principle of the sending country's freedom to appoint members of the diplomatic mission, and all that is required of this country should do is notify the host country of the full name, grade, and rank of the consular officer in advance and sufficient time, so that the host country can, if it so desires, declare him persona non grata.

The host country has the right to restrict the size of the consular mission within the limits of what it deems reasonable and normal in view of the circumstances and conditions existing in the jurisdiction of the consulate and in view of the needs of the consular mission, in the event that there is no express agreement between the two countries stipulating a specific number, and Article (22) of the Relationship Agreement does not allow the consulate may appoint consular staff from among the nationals of the host country only after obtaining its express consent, which it may withdraw at any time.

Circle of consular jurisdiction

A consular jurisdiction circle is defined as "the area designated for a consular mission to exercise its consular functions in it." And unlike what is being done in diplomatic relations in that the sending country does not establish only one diplomatic mission in the host country, its headquarters is usually in the capital.

Often, consular posts are established in various regions within the host country, because of their commercial, industrial, or economic importance, or because they contain a large number of nationals of the sending country, or from communities with which they have national or ethnic ties, therefore, there is an urgent need to determine the geographical area in which the mission is exercised.

The consulate includes its competencies and functions, which is what the Vienna Convention on Consular Relations called the consular jurisdiction circle.

Based on the foregoing, the circle of consular jurisdiction may extend to the territory of the host country as a whole, which is the case in which the sending country has only one consular mission in the host country, or when consular functions are undertaken by the diplomatic mission of the sending country due to the latter not establishing a consular mission in the host country.

The consular jurisdiction circle or consular area may be limited to a part of the host country's territory when the latter's territory is divided into many consular areas, each of which has a specific consular mission established by the sending country with the consent and agreement of the host country.

The headquarters of the consular mission and its jurisdiction are determined by the sending country, after the approval of the host country, and if the sending country wishes to make any subsequent modification to the headquarters of its consular residence or to the jurisdictional area, it must obtain the approval of the host country, and the representative of the consulate may be forced in some special circumstances, such as emergency circumstances, to exercise his consular duties outside the area of jurisdiction of his consular mission.

The Vienna Convention on Consular Relations dealt with this case, requiring the consent of the host country to be obtained before the consular officer moves outside the jurisdiction of his mission.

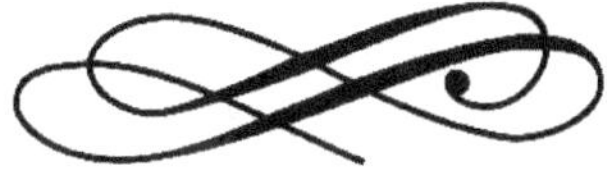

Consular functions

Although the appointment of consuls and the establishment of consular missions are mainly in order to take care of the country's commercial, industrial, and economic interests related to navigation, international dealings settled on assigning other functions to the consuls. Therefore, international norms, consular and commercial agreements, national laws, regulations, and instructions for consular work included detailed rules dealing with the functions and tasks of consuls.

Article (5) of the Vienna Convention of 1963 included a number of consular functions, which are:

1- Protecting the interests of the citizens of the sending country within the limits required by international law.

2- Developing commercial, economic, cultural, and scientific relations between the sending and hosting countries

3- To inquire, identify and submit reports on the commercial, economic, cultural, and scientific conditions in the host country.

4- Issuing passports and travel documents for citizens of the sending country. Granting entry visas and travel documents to foreigners.

5- Providing aid to the citizens of the sending country.

6- Doing the work of a notary public, registering civil status, and carrying out some administrative work and similar jobs to the extent permitted by the laws of the host country.

7- Protecting and looking after the interests of the country's citizens in inheritance and succession cases in accordance with the laws of the host country.

8- Protecting the interests of minors, incapacitated persons, and detainees who are citizens of the sending country within the limits of the laws of the host country.

9- Representing the citizens of the sending country or taking decisions and measures to secure their representation in front of the courts or authorities of the host country in accordance with the applicable laws of this country. And to seek, in accordance with the laws of the host country, and provisional measures to preserve the rights and interests of such persons, when they are not able, due to their absence or for any other reason, to defend their rights and interests in a timely manner.

10- Transferring or delivering papers, documents, judicial and non-judicial notifications, and executing rogatory representations and hearing costs for testimony on behalf of the courts of the sending country in accordance with applicable international agreements. And in the absence of such agreements, in any way consistent with the laws of the host country.

11- Exercising the rights of control and inspection on ships and aircraft that bear the nationality of the sending country and on the crew of their navigators in accordance with the laws in force in the host country.

12- To provide assistance and aid to ships and aircraft that bear the nationality of the sending country and to their navigators, and to settle disputes between the captain, officers, and sailors within the limits permitted by the laws of the sending country. Article (5) of the Vienna Convention of 1963 added to the aforementioned functions the exercise of any other function entrusted by the sending country to the consular mission and which is consistent with the laws of the host country, or is not objected to by this country, or is included in the international agreements in force between the sending and hosting countries. It is evident from this addition that the consular functions specified in Article (5) of the Vienna Convention of 1963 are not exclusive.

Consular functions accommodate any other function that may be based on consular missions in the case where the sending country does not have a diplomatic mission in the host country or is not represented therein by a diplomatic mission of a third country, with diplomatic duties and functions, provided that the host country agrees to that, and the consul carrying out these functions does not affect his consular character. It also does not entitle him to diplomatic immunities and privileges.

Consular relations do not differ from diplomatic relations in the possibility of performing the function of double or multiple representations. With regard to double representation, Article (7) of the Vienna Convention on Consular Relations permitted the sending country, after notifying the concerned countries and not expressly objecting from one of them, to assign a consular mission present in a particular country, exercising consular functions in another country.

The agreement permitted another form of double or multiple representations that differs from the first form in that the latter mission exercises jurisdiction outside the territory of its host country, while the other form is based on the idea of representation of the consular mission as a spatial extension in the jurisdiction, where it exercises consular functions for the benefit of two or more countries, i.e. one country exercises the functions has after notifying the host country without objection.

It was noted that the second form of dual representation does not require an explicit objection on the part of the host country, as is the case with the first form. In conclusion, it should be noted that the General Assembly of the United Nations considered in 1990 the adoption of an additional protocol to the Vienna Convention of 1963 related to consular functions, and after the General Assembly explored the views of countries on the protocol, it became clear to it that the issue did not enjoy the support or wide interest of the countries, and the General Assembly removed the issue of the protocol from its agenda in 1992.

Consular immunities and privileges

Consuls do not enjoy the same legal status as diplomatic envoys, as they are not representatives of their countries in all their international relations, and although they are appointed by a foreign country and granted consular licenses, they are not representatives of their countries as is the case with diplomatic envoys, as the host country recognizes them as agents of the sending country to carry out specific tasks and for local purposes only.

In order for consuls and members of consular missions to carry out their work and functions, protection must be provided for them, and this protection is in fact consistent with the nature and limits of their jobs, especially since they are appointed for local or internal purposes, which means that their links and relations within the host country are direct with the internal or local authorities of the host country

If the consular missions wish to deal with the central authorities of this country, it is natural for them to resort to that through their diplomatic mission located on the territory of the host country, to which the consular mission itself is subject.

Customary international law does not contain comprehensive rules regarding consular privileges and immunities. Therefore, the Vienna Convention on Consular

Relations is the most comprehensive and complete international instrument in this field.

Although the agreement recognized the principle of special protection for consular missions and their members, international norms and global convention rules do not include any legal provision that makes consular missions identical or equivalent in terms of consular immunities and privileges.

Article (40) of the Vienna Convention on Consular Relations of 1963 includes what confirms this idea because it requires the host country to treat consular members with the necessary respect for them and take all appropriate measures to protect them and to prevent any infringement on their person, freedom, or dignity.

Therefore, consular immunities and privileges and the inviolability of consular premises are well-established principles of international law. However, the difference in the nature of consular duties from diplomacy inevitably justifies the different legal status of consuls from diplomatic envoys.

It is noted that consular immunities and privileges were very narrow and limited in the nineteenth century, and the protection and giving of consuls took special treatment and a more important and broader dimension after that, but their legal status, immunities, and privileges are still less than what is recognized for diplomatic missions, whether in terms of quantity and quality.

It is indeed hoped that the Vienna Convention on Consular Relations of 1963 will contribute to creating unified and generally accepted behavior regarding consular immunities and privileges, which today has become a reality for some provisions and not just a hope or expectation, these provisions that have become part of customary international law include the following:

A- Immunities and privileges approved by the Vienna Convention on Consular Relations in favor of career consuls are equivalent to diplomatic immunities and privileges in terms of their nature, although they are less extensive in terms of their scope. The Vienna Convention on Consular Relations established personal immunity and inviolability for consular staff, which is what the Vienna Convention on Diplomatic Relations did for diplomatic envoys, but the scope of immunity and personal inviolability in the second agreement is wider than the scope of similar immunity contained in the first agreement.

The scope of the immunity and personal inviolability of the consular staff is limited to the inadmissibility of arresting or detaining him except by a decision issued by the judicial authority in connection with a serious felony, provided that the sending country is informed. As for the personal inviolability of the diplomatic envoy as stated in Article (29) of the Vienna Convention on Diplomatic Relations, it is absolute. As for honorary consuls, it can be said that the general principle is that they do not enjoy immunities and privileges and that the limited immunities recognized for them are an exception to this principle, as the immunities prescribed for them in the Consular Relations Agreement are less than what is granted to career consuls.

B - The consular staff and members are not subject to the jurisdiction of the judicial and administrative authorities of the host country with regard to the work and activities they perform related to the conduct of their consular activities and functions.

Therefore, Article (42/2) of the Vienna Convention on Consular Relations made an exception to the aforementioned judicial immunity, as it made the judicial and administrative authorities of the host country competent to consider civil cases in two cases:

If it results from a contract concluded by a member, consular officer, or employee without it being expressly or implicitly concluded by him in his capacity as a representative of the sending country, or if it is raised by a third party for damage arising from an accident in the host country caused by a vehicle, ship or aircraft.

C- The consular employee or member does not enjoy penal immunity against the host country, contrary to what has been settled for the diplomatic envoy. In this regard, Article (41) of the Vienna Convention on Consular Relations approved the subjection of consuls to the penal jurisdiction of the host country and specified the procedures to be followed when prosecuting, arresting, or trying to maintain their legal status within the host country.

The aforementioned article stipulates that the consuls must appear in front of the national penal authorities, and they may not be subjected to arrest or detention unless the crime committed is a serious felony and after a decision is issued by the competent court in this regard.

During the implementation of a final judicial decision, and if the consular member appears in front of the competent court, the trial procedures must be conducted with the necessary respect for him, respecting his official position and in a way that does not hinder the exercise of his consular duties except to the least possible extent.

D- Consular Premises enjoy immunity and inviolability to the extent necessary to carry out consular functions. The authorities of the host country cannot enter part of the consular buildings or premises for consular work without the approval of the head of the consular post, and this approval is presumed in case of fire or in any other case, or another emergency calls for immediate judicial measures.

The consular buildings are also immune from seizure for the purposes of national defense or public benefit, and the host country is obligated to protect the consular buildings. The Vienna Convention on Consular Relations stipulates a text dealing with this issue, and the conferees unanimously agreed to grant consular missions such a right, but the agreement did not include a text on this issue because the Vienna Convention on Diplomatic Relations of 1961 was also devoid of a text related to this subject.

E- The inviolability of consular archives and functions is one of the basic rules regulating consular work under customary international law. Article (33) of the Vienna Convention on Consular Relations of 1963 clearly recognized this inviolability, stressing that consular archives and documents are inviolable at all times and wherever they are.

The consular archives mean "all papers, documents, correspondence, books, pens, tapes, records of the consular mission, as well as symbol tools, index cards and any part of the furniture used for their maintenance and preservation." goes under the inviolability of the archives. Documents, and official correspondence of the consular mission, as all correspondence related to the consular mission, enjoy complete inviolability and confidentiality.

In addition, the consular pouch may not be opened or seized, and if the host country has serious reasons to believe that the pouch is being used for purposes other than those intended for it, it may request that it be opened in its presence by an authorized representative of the sending country. If the authorities of the sending country reject the request, it may the host country shall return the bag to its source.

F- Consular employees and members, and members of their families who live with them in the same living quarters, are exempted from all personal, civil, local and municipal taxes and fees. They also enjoy exemption from a number of customs duties, taxes, and other additional fees. These persons are exempted, in accordance with the provisions of Articles (46) and (47) of the Vienna Convention on Consular Relations, from all restrictions imposed within the host country regarding the registration of foreigners, residence permits, work permits, and any obligations related thereto. They arc also exempted from the provisions of social insurance, from personal and public services of any nature, and from military obligations.

G- The Vienna Convention on Consular Relations did not exclude the members of the consular mission from testifying in front of the courts of the host country, as it allowed them to be asked to give their testimonies during the course of judicial or administrative procedures, and it did not allow employees or consular members to refuse to give their testimonies except for facts that are directly related to their work. They are also not obligated to submit documents and official correspondence related to these facts.

They may also decline to testify in their capacity as experts on the national law of their sending country, and if the consular officer refuses to testify in cases other than those mentioned, no compulsory or punitive action shall be taken against him. In all cases, the party wishing to hear the testimony of the consular officer must avoid obstructing his consular duties and functions, and it can obtain his testimony at his residence or consular mission or through a written report submitted to it. It is worth noting that honorary consular employees enjoy part of the previous immunities and privileges, which are few in number and do not extend to their family members, nor do family members of any consular employee working in a consular mission headed by an honorary consul benefit from them.

In conclusion, it must be said that the members of the consular mission enjoy, according to the text of Article 53 of the Vienna Convention on Consular Relations, the immunities and privileges prescribed for them as soon as they enter the territory of the host country with the intention of reaching their place of work, and as soon as he takes over his work in the consular mission if he is present initially in the territory of the host country. As for the members of his family who live with him, they shall enjoy the immunities and privileges recognized for them as of their entry into the territory of the host country or from the date on which they became members of the family of the consular member

Termination of the consular function

Article (25) of the Vienna Convention on Consular Relations stipulates that the duties of a member of a consular post usually end with the following:

(a) A declaration by the sending country to the host country of the termination of his duties.

(b) Withdrawal of consular exequatur.

(c) A notification from the host country to the sending country that it no longer considers the concerned person a member of the consular staff.

(d) The reasons for the termination of the consular function are mentioned in the text of Article (25) of the Vienna Convention on Consular Relations:

1- Declaration of termination of consular capacity by the sending country

It is obvious and logical that the country appoints the consuls and gives them their powers and authority, and it is the sending country of course that has the authority to supervise them and monitor the performance of their work and tasks entrusted to them, and the same applies to their transfer, acceptance of their resignation and dispensation of their services.

The consular employee or member does not lose his consular capacity vis-à-vis the host country as soon as the decision to terminate his consular work is issued by the sending country, but he continues to enjoy it until the host country is notified of the termination of his consular work.

2- Withdrawal of consular exequatur

The host country has the right at any time to withdraw its consent expressed in the consular exequatur for a person to exercise consular functions within its territory, the withdrawal of consular exequatur may take the form of ***"cancellation of the consular exequatur, deportation or expulsion of the consular officer" or "request to withdraw the consular employee."***

No matter how different these formulas are in terms of naming, they have one result, which is the host country's withdrawal of its consent for a person to exercise consular functions over its territory.

Risks are represented in the intervention of the consular officer concerned with the internal affairs of the host country, in the practice of espionage against it, or in the wrong exercise calling the intervention of police or judicial powers of the host country, or in the conspiracy against the host country or in the abuse of immunities and consular privileges.

3- Notification of non-considering the concerned person from the consular staff

The text of Article (25/C) of the Vienna Convention on Consular Relations of 1963 is closely related to the text of Article (23) of the same Convention "persona non grata" or that any member of the consular staff is deemed inadmissible, and the sending country shall, in this case, summon the person concerned or terminate his duties with this mission as the case may be.

If the sending country refuses to recall the person concerned or to terminate his duties within a reasonable period, the host country may withdraw the consular exequatur granted to the person concerned or cease to consider him as a member of the consular staff.

The host country is not obligated to explain the reasons that prompted it not to consider a person a member of the consular staff, and by adopting this provision, the Vienna Convention on Consular Relations enshrined the rules stipulated in Article (9) of the Vienna Convention on Diplomatic Relations, which included a similar provision regarding members of diplomatic missions.

4- *Reasons not included in the Vienna Convention*

In addition to the reasons provided in the Vienna Convention on Consular Relations for the termination of consular work, there are reasons that may lead to the termination of consular work that is not mentioned in the Vienna Convention, and these reasons are:

A- Death of a member of the consular post

The death of a consular member is one of the natural causes leading to the termination of the consular mission entrusted to him. The Havana Convention of 1928 (Article 23/a) contained a provision dealing with this issue. As for the Vienna Convention on Consular Relations of 1963, it did not explicitly refer to the death of a mission member. However, Article (53/5) of it included a legal provision that explicitly deals with the status of family members of the consular mission in the event of his death, as it stipulated that family members of the consular mission upon his death if they lived under his protection, continue to enjoy the immunities and privileges granted to them until their departure territory of the host country or until the expiration of a reasonable period enabling them to do so, whichever is earlier.

B- Disappearance of one or both countries

The status of the consul is established for a person through the sending and host countries, and therefore this capacity will inevitably disappear with the disappearance of one of these two countries or with their disappearance together, but the reality of consular dealings reveals cases in which the disappearance of the sending country did not lead to the loss of the member of the consular mission of his official capacity in a number from the host countries.

In some of these cases, the order of the consul whose country he was working for ceased to be subject to the internal law of the host country, and it is expected that this situation will be affected by several political factors, for example, their disappearance or their loss of sovereignty results in moving to another country, ending the mission of the member of the consular mission, unless the successor country which is the country that replaced the predecessor country in sovereignty over the territory after its disappearance, issues a new consular exequatur or temporary permission in favor of the career member.

C- Severing diplomatic or consular relations and closing consular missions

It is established in international consular law that war does not inevitably or necessarily lead to the cessation or severance of consular relations between the sending and host countries, and the same applies to the severing of diplomatic relations. It is necessary to sever consular relations, especially since the representative capacity is not one of the requirements for consular work.

If it happens that consular relations between the sending and host countries are severed for any reason whatsoever, the host country, even if the reason for the severance of relations is an armed conflict, is obligated to protect the consular premises, property, archives, and records of the sending country, and the sending country may entrust the protection of its consular premises, assets, and archives to a third country on condition the approval of the host country, and all the aforementioned provisions apply in cases of permanent or temporary suspension of a consular post.

References

*- James Rosenau Comparing Foreign Policies, Why, What, How In James Rosenau, Comparing Foreign Policies (N. Y. Hassled press, 1974).

*- Jan Brawn lie, Principles of Public International Law, Oxford: Oxford University Press, 2003.

*- B. S. Murty, The International Law of Diplomacy. The Diplomatic Instrument and World Public Order, Dordrecht: Martinus Neuhoff Publish- errs, 1989.

*- Ernest Stow, A Guide to Diplomatic Practice, 4th. ed edited by Neville Bland London: Longmans, Green and Co, 1958.

*- George Modelski, A Theory of Foreign Policy, New York: Praeger, 1962. Hans Morgenthau, Politics Among Nations, New York, Alfred knop 1971.

*- C. Clapman W. Walesa (ed) Foreign Policy Making In Developing States, West med Saxon House 1977.

*- Brad Roth, Governmental Illegitimacy in International Law, Oxford: Ox- ford University Press, 2000.

*- Krueger(ed), The WTO as an International Organization, 1998; Jackson, "The World Trade Organization: Constitution and Jurisprudence", 1998.

*- J.K Subenius, Negotiation the Law of the Sea, Harvard University Press, 1984.

*- Paul Ekins, A New World Order Grassroots Movements for Global Change, London, Routledge 1992.

*- M. Dixon and R. McCorquodale, Cases and Materials on International Law, Oxford: Oxford University Press, 2003.

*- J. pinder, "Economic Diplomacy" in James N. Rosenau and others, World Polities, New York, The free press, 1976, P. 338.

9 798372 093317